FOUR

AMERICAN NAVAL HEROES

PAUL JONES ADMIRAL FARRAGUT
OLIVER H. PERRY ADMIRAL DEWEY

A BOOK FOR YOUNG AMERICANS

BY MABEL BORTON BEEBE

WITH AN INTRODUCTION BY JAMES BALDWIN

WERNER SCHOOL BOOK COMPANY

NEW YORK CHICAGO BOSTON

THE

FOUR GREAT AMERICANS SERIES

**Biographical Stories of Great Americans
for Young Americans**

EDITED BY

JAMES BALDWIN, Ph.D.

IN these biographical stories the lives of great Americans are presented in such a manner as to hold the attention of the youngest reader. In these lives the child finds the most inspiring examples of good citizenship and true patriotism.

VOLUMES NOW READY:

I. FOUR GREAT AMERICANS

George Washington, Benjamin Franklin, Daniel Webster, Abraham Lincoln.
By JAMES BALDWIN, Ph.D.

Cloth, 246 pages   ✓   ✓   ✓   Price, 50 cents

II. FOUR AMERICAN PATRIOTS

Patrick Henry, Alexander Hamilton, Andrew Jackson, U. S. Grant.
By ALMA HOLMAN BURTON
Author of The Story of Our Country, etc.

Cloth, 256 pages   ✓   ✓   ✓   Price, 50 cents

III. FOUR AMERICAN NAVAL HEROES

Paul Jones, Oliver H. Perry, Admiral Farragut, Admiral Dewey.
By MABEL BORTON BEEBE

Cloth, 254 pages   ✓   ✓   ✓   Price, 50 cents

OTHER VOLUMES IN PREPARATION

CONTENTS

THE STORY OF OLIVER H. PERRY

THE STORY OF ADMIRAL FARRAGUT

THE STORY OF ADMIRAL DEWEY

INTRODUCTION.

Four times in the history of our country has the American navy achieved renown and won the gratitude of the nation. These four times correspond, of course, to the four great wars that we have had ; and with the mention of each the name of a famous hero of the sea is at once brought to mind. What would the Revolution have been without its Paul Jones; or the War of 1812, without its Perry? How differently might the Civil War have ended but for its Farragut ; and

SEAL OF THE
U. S. NAVY.

the Spanish War, but for its Dewey! The story of the achievements of these four men covers a large part of our naval history.

Six months after the battle of Lexington the Continental Congress decided to raise and equip a fleet to help carry on the war against England. Before the end of the year (1775) seventeen vessels were ready for service, and it was then that Paul Jones began his public career. Many other ships were soon added.

The building and equipping of this first navy was largely intrusted to Ezek Hopkins, whom Congress had appointed Commander-in-Chief, but it does not seem that he did all that was expected of him, for within less than two years

EZEK HOPKINS.

he was dismissed. He was the only person who ever held the title of Commander-in-Chief of the navy. During the war several other vessels were added to the fleet, and over 800 prizes were captured from the British. But before peace was declared twenty-four of our ships had been taken by the enemy, others had been wrecked in storms, and nearly all the rest were disabled. There was no effort to build other vessels, and so, for many years, our country had no navy.

In 1794, when war with the Barbary States was expected, Congress ordered the building of six large frigates. One of these was the famous *Constitution,* which is still in existence and about which Dr. Holmes wrote the well-known

THE FRIGATE CONSTITUTION.

poem called "Old Ironsides."

Through all the earlier years of our history, John Adams used his influence to strengthen our power on the sea; and he was so far successful that he has often been called "The Father of the American Navy." When the War of 1812 began the United States owned a great many gunboats for coast defense, besides seventeen sea-going vessels. It was during this war that the navy especially distinguished itself, and Oliver Hazard Perry made his name famous.

A SLOOP OF WAR.

The ships of war in those earlier times were wooden sailing vessels, and they were very slow-goers when compared with the swift cruisers which sail the ocean now. The largest of these vessels were called ships of the line, because they formed the line of battle in any general fight at sea. They usually had three decks, with guns on every deck. The upper deck was often covered over, and on the open deck thus formed above there was a fourth tier of guns. This open deck was called the forecastle and quarter-deck. Some of the largest ships of the line carried as many as 120 guns each; the smallest was built to carry 72 guns.

Next in size to these ships were the frigates. A frigate had only one covered deck and the open forecastle and quarter-deck above it, and therefore had but two tiers of guns. The largest frigate carried sixty guns, besides a large pivot gun at the bow. The American frigates were noted for their speed.

Still smaller than the frigates were the corvettes, or sloops of war, as they are more commonly called. These had but one tier of guns, and that was on the open deck. They were rigged like the larger vessels, with three masts and square sails.

THE STEAM FRIGATE POWHATAN.

The fourth class of vessels included the brigs of war, which had but two masts and carried from six to twenty guns. Equal to them in size were the schooners, which also had two masts, but were rigged fore-and-aft. The guns which they carried were commonly much smaller than those on the sloops and frigates.

After Robert Fulton's invention of the steamboat in 1807 there were many attempts to apply steam on vessels of war. But it was a long time before these attempts were very successful. The earliest war steamships were driven by paddle-wheels, placed at the sides of the vessels. The paddles, besides taking up much valuable space, were exposed to the shots of the enemy, and in any battle were very easily crippled and made useless. But the speed of these vessels was much greater than that of any sailing ship, and this alone made them very desirable. For many

THE MERRIMAC AND THE MONITOR.

years steam frigates were the most formidable vessels in the navy. The first successful steamship of war was the English frigate *Penelope*, which was built in 1843, and carried forty-six guns. One of the earliest and most noted American vessels of the same type was the *Powhatan*. The first screw line of battle ship was built by the French in 1849. It was called the *Napoleon*, and carried one hundred guns. It was so successful that steamships soon began to take the place of sailing vessels in all the navies of the world.

Up to this time all war vessels were built of wood ; but

there had been many experiments to learn whether they might not be protected by iron plating. The first iron-clad ship was built in France in 1858 ; and not long after that Great Britain added to her navy an entire fleet of iron-clads. All these were built after the same pattern as wooden ships, and were simply covered or protected with iron plates.

The first iron-clads used in our own navy were built soon after the beginning of the Civil War (1861), and were designed for use on the large rivers and along the coast.

THE BATTLESHIP OREGON.

They were called "turtle-backs," and were simply large steamboats covered with thick slabs of iron and carrying thirteen guns each. The iron slabs were joined closely together and laid in such a manner as to inclose the decks with sloping sides and roofs. The first great deviation from old patterns was the *Monitor*, built by John Ericsson in 1862. She was the strangest looking craft that had ever been seen, and has been likened to a big washtub turned upside down and floating on the water. The *Merrimac*, which she defeated in Hampton Roads, was a wooden frigate which the Confederates had made into an iron-clad by covering her with railroad rails. They had also, by giving her an iron prow, converted her into a ram. These two vessels, the *Monitor* and the *Merrimac*, were indirectly the cause of a great revolution in naval warfare ; they were the forerunners of all the modern ships of war now in existence. The nations of the world saw at once that there would be no more use for ships of the line and wooden frigates and sloops of war.

The ships that have been built since that time are entirely unlike those with which Paul Jones and Commodore Perry and Admiral Farragut won their great victories. The largest and most formidable of the new vessels are known as battleships, and may be briefly described as floating forts, built of

THE DYNAMITE CRUISER VESUVIUS.

steel and armed with powerful guns. These are named after the states, as the *Oregon*, the *Texas*, and the *Iowa*. Next to them in importance are the great monitors, such as the *Monadnock* and the *Monterey*. These are slow sailers but terrible fighters, and are intended chiefly for harbor defense. The cruisers, which rank next, are smaller than battleships and are not so heavily armed ; but they are built for speed, and their swiftness makes up for their lack of strength. Among the most noted of these are the *Brooklyn*, the *Columbia*, and the *Minneapolis*. There are also smaller cruisers, such as the *Cincinnati* and the *Raleigh*, that are intended rather for scout duty than for service in battle. Most of the cruisers are named after cities. One of the strangest vessels in the navy is the dynamite cruiser *Vesuvius*, which is armed with terrible dynamite guns. Then there is the ram *Katahdin*. She carries no heavy guns, and her only weapon of offense is a powerful ram. Her speed is greater than that of most battleships, and she is protected by a covering of the heaviest steel armor. Besides all these there are a number of smaller vessels, such as torpedo boats and tugs.

A few old-fashioned wooden vessels—steam frigates and sailing vessels—are still to be found in our navy yards, but these would be of no use in a battle.

In reading of the exploits of our great naval heroes it is well to keep in mind these wonderful changes that have taken place in the navy. Think of the slow-going wooden frigates which sailed the seas in the time of Paul Jones or Commodore Perry—how small and insignificant they would be if placed side by side with the tremendous *Oregon* or with the cruisers which Admiral Dewey led to victory in the Bay of Manila! But if the glory of an achievement is measured by the difficulties that are encountered and overcome, to whom shall we award the greater honor—to our earlier heroes, or to our later?   JAMES BALDWIN.

THE STORY OF

PAUL JONES

THE STORY OF PAUL JONES.

I.—THE LITTLE SCOTCH LAD.

Many years ago there lived, in the southwestern part of Scotland, on the beautiful bay called Solway Firth, a gentleman whose name was Mr. Craik. In Scotland, a large farm is called an estate. Mr. Craik named his estate Arbigland.

His large house stood high on the shore overlooking the sea. The lawn sloped gradually to the firth.

Mr. Craik's gardener, John Paul, lived in a cottage on the estate. Mr. Craik was very fond of John Paul, for he worked well. He made the grounds like a beautiful park, and planted many trees, some of which are still standing.

One day John Paul married Jean Macduff. She was the daughter of a neighboring farmer. She and John lived very happily in their little cottage. They had seven children. The fifth child was a boy, named for his father, John Paul. He was born July 6, 1747.

When little John was large enough to run about he liked to play on the beautiful lawn and to wander along the shore of the firth. Sometimes he would sit still for hours watching the waves.

Sometimes he and Mr. Craik's little boy would play with tiny sailboats and paddle about in the water. When they grew tired of this, they would climb among the rocks on the mountains which were back of the estate.

When there were storms at sea, vessels would come into Solway Firth for a safe harbor. The water was very deep near the shore. Because of this the ships could come so near the lawn of Arbigland that their masts seemed to touch the overhanging trees.

Little John Paul and his playmates liked to watch the sailors, and sometimes could even talk to them. They heard many wonderful stories of a land called America, where grew the tobacco that was packed in some of the ships.

The children would often take their little sailboats to some inlet, where they would play sailor.
John Paul was always the captain.   He had list-
ened carefully to the commands given by the
captains of the large vessels.   These he would
repeat correctly and with great dignity, though he
did not always understand them.

John Paul spent more time in this kind of play
than in going to school.   In those days there were
few schools, and book-learning was not thought to
be of much use.   At a parish school near by, John
learned to spell and to repeat the rules of gram-
mar.

When he was twelve years old he felt that the
time had come when he could be a real sailor.   So
his father allowed him to go across the firth to an
English town called Whitehaven.   There he was
apprenticed to Mr. Younger, a merchant, who
owned a ship and traded in goods brought from
foreign lands.

He soon went to sea in Mr. Younger's vessel,
the *Friendship*.   This ship was bound for America to get tobacco from the Virginia fields.

II.—THE YOUNG SAILOR.

At that time the trip across the Atlantic could not be made as quickly as now. There were no steamships, and the sailing vessels had, of course, to depend upon the wind to carry them to their destination. It was several months before the *Friendship* anchored at the mouth of the Rappahannock River.

Farther inland, on this river, was the town of Fredericksburg. John Paul's eldest brother, William, lived there. He had left his Scottish home many years before, and had come with his wife to Virginia. Here he was now living on his own plantation, where he raised tobacco for the English market.

While the *Friendship* was in port being loaded for its return voyage, John Paul went to Fredericksburg to stay with his brother. While there he spent the most of his time in hard study. Although he was still young, he had found that he could not succeed as he wished with so little education.

It was during these months in America that he

formed the habit of study. All through the remainder of his life his leisure time was given to the reading of books.

After he returned to Scotland he spent six years in the employ of Mr. Younger. During that time he learned a great deal about good seamanship.

When John Paul was nineteen years of age, the loss of money compelled Mr. Younger to give up his business.

John Paul was soon afterward made mate on a slaver called the *Two Friends*. This was a vessel whose sole business was the carrying of slaves from Africa to America and other countries.

People at that time did not think there was any wrong in slave-trading. It was a very profitable business. Even the sailors made more money than did those on vessels engaged in any other business.

The *Two Friends* carried a cargo of slaves to Jamaica, an English possession in the West Indies. As soon as port was reached, John Paul left the vessel. He said that he would never again sail on a slave-trading voyage. He could not endure to see men and women treated so cruelly, and bought and sold like cattle.

He sailed for home as a passenger on board a small trading vessel. On the voyage both the captain and the mate died of fever, and the ship with all its passengers was in mid-ocean with no one to command.

John Paul took the captain's place, for no one else knew so much about seamanship. This was a daring thing for one so young, as he was not yet twenty years old.

When he brought the vessel safely into port, the owners were so grateful to him that they made him the captain.

Soon afterward he sailed for the West Indies. The carpenter on board was, one day, very disrespectful to the young captain. He was punished by a flogging, and was discharged. Not long after this he died of a fever.

The enemies of John Paul, who were jealous of him, thought this was their chance to do him harm. They said that the flogging had killed the carpenter.

Many people believed this, and when John Paul again returned to Scotland, he found that his friends had lost their faith in him.

During the next two years he made several voyages, but all the while he remembered the injustice done to him. He finally succeeded, however, in proving to his friends that he was worthy of their confidence.

III.—THE BEGINNING OF THE AMERICAN REVOLUTION.

When John Paul visited his brother in Virginia, America was not much like what it is now. Most of the country was an unexplored wilderness, and there was no United States as we know it to-day.

Some large settlements, known as colonies, had been made in that part of the country which lies between the Atlantic Ocean and the Alleghany Mountains.

Most of the people who lived in these colonies were English, and their governors were appointed by the king of England.

Each governor, with the help of a few men whom he chose from the people, would make laws for the colony.

Not all the laws were made in this way. Sometimes the king, without caring for the wishes of the colonists, would make laws to suit himself.

Up to this time the people had been obedient and loyal to their king. But when George the Third came to the throne of England, he caused the people a great deal of trouble.

He sent orders to the governors that the colonists should trade with no other country than his own.

All their goods should be bought in England, and, to pay for them, they must send to the same country all the corn, cotton, and tobacco which they had to sell. The colonists wished to build factories and weave their own cloth, but the king would not allow this.

For a long while England had been at war with France. King George said that the colonists should help pay the expenses of that war, and therefore he began to tax them heavily.

They were obliged to pay a tax on every pound of tea, and stamped paper must be bought for every legal document.

The colonists were much aroused on account of the tea tax and the stamp act, as it was called.

One day startling news came to John Paul in Virginia. A shipload of tea had anchored in Boston harbor. The colonists declared that they would not pay the tax on this tea, and some of them, dressed as Indians, had gone on board the vessel and thrown it all into the harbor.

Later on, came the news that the king had sent his English soldiers to Boston to keep the people quiet. He had also closed the port of Boston and said that no more ships should come in or go out. This aroused the whole country. Everybody felt that something must be done to preserve the freedom of the people.

Each colony chose men as delegates to confer together about what was best to be done. The delegates met in Philadelphia on the 5th of September, 1774. That meeting has since been called the First Continental Congress of America.

The delegates of the colonies decided to send a petition to the king asking that he would remove the taxes and not make unjust laws.

All winter the people waited for an answer, but as none came, matters grew worse in the spring.

On the 19th of April, 1775, a battle was fought with the king's soldiers at Lexington, in Massachusetts. This was the first battle of the American Revolution.

IV.—PAUL JONES.

In the year 1773, soon after the trouble with England had begun, John Paul's brother William died in Virginia. He left some money and his plantation, but had made no will to say who should have them. He had no children, and his wife had been dead for years.

His father had died the year before, and John was the only one of the family now living who could manage the estate.

So he left the sea and went to live on the farm near Fredericksburg, in Virginia. He thought that he would spend the rest of his life in the quiet country, and never return to the sea.

He soon learned to love America very dearly, even more than he did his own country. He wanted to see the colonists win in their struggle for their rights.

But so good a sailor could not be a good farmer. In two years the farm was in a bad condition and all the money left by his brother had been spent. The agents in Scotland, with whom John Paul had left money for the care of his mother and sisters, had proved to be dishonest, and this money also had been lost.

In the midst of these perplexities, he decided to serve America in the war which every one saw was now inevitable.

Another congress of delegates from the colonies met in 1775, and made preparations for that war. The colonists were organized into an army, with George Washington as the commander in chief.

A fleet of English vessels had been sent across the Atlantic. The swiftest of these sailed up and down the Atlantic coast, forcing the people in the

towns to give provisions to the king's sailors and
soldiers.   Other vessels were constantly coming
over, loaded with arms and ammunition for the
English soldiers.

George Washington's army was almost without

ammunition.   There was
very little gunpowder made
in this country at that
time, and the need of it
was very great.

It was thought that the
best way to supply the
American army with am-
munition was to capture
the English vessels. It was

JOHN ADAMS.

for this purpose that the first American navy was
organized.

The first navy yard was established at Plymouth.   Here a few schooners and merchant vessels were equipped with cannon as warships.
These were manned by bold, brave men, who,
since boyhood, had been on the sea in fishing or
trading vessels.

No member of the Continental Congress did more to strengthen and enlarge this first navy than John Adams.

In 1775 John Paul settled up his affairs, left the Virginia farm, and went to Philadelphia to offer his services to the naval committee of Congress.

He gave his name as John Paul Jones. Just why he did this, we do not know. Perhaps he did not wish his friends in Scotland to know that he had taken up arms against his native country.

Perhaps he thought that, should he ever be captured by the English, it would go harder with him if they should know his English name. We cannot tell. Hereafter we shall call him Paul Jones, as this is the name by which he was known during the rest of his life.

Congress accepted his offer and he was made first lieutenant on the *Alfred*, a flag-ship.

V.—THE CRUISE OF THE ALFRED.

The young lieutenant was now twenty-nine years old. His health was excellent and he could

endure great fatigue.   His figure was light, grace-
ful, and active.   His face was stern and his manner was soldierly.   He was a fine seaman and
familiar with armed vessels.

He knew that the men placed above him in
the navy had had less experience than he.   But

THE PINE TREE FLAG.

he took the position given him
without complaint.

When the commander of the
Alfred came on board, Paul Jones
hoisted the American flag.   This
was the first time a flag of our
own had ever been raised.

We do not know just what this flag was like,
but some of the earliest naval flags bore the
picture of a pine tree; others had a rattlesnake
stretched across the stripes, and the words, ''Don't
tread on me.''   Our present flag was not adopted
until two years later.

On the 17th of February, 1776, the first American squadron sailed for the Bahama Islands.

On the way, two British sloops were captured.
The English sailors told the Americans that on the

island of New Providence were forts, which con-
tained a large amount of military supplies. They
said that these forts could easily be taken.

The soldiers on a vessel are called marines.
A plan was made to hide the American marines
in the British sloops. In that way it was thought
they could go safely into the harbor of New
Providence. Then they could land
and take possession of the forts.

This plan would have been
successful, but for one foolish mis-
take. The squadron sailed so
close to the harbor during the
night that in the morning all the

THE RATTLESNAKE
FLAG.

ships could be seen from the shore. The war vessels should have remained out of sight until the
marines had been safely landed from the sloops.
The alarm was spread, and the sloops were not
allowed to cross the bar.

The commander of the squadron then planned
to land on the opposite side of the island and
take the forts from the rear, but Paul Jones
told him he could not do this. There was no

place to anchor the squadron, and no road to the forts.

However, he had learned from the pilots of a good landing nor far from the harbor. When he told the commander of this, he was only rebuked for confiding in pilots.

So Paul Jones undertook, alone, to conduct the *Alfred* to the landing he had found. He succeeded in doing this and the whole squadron afterwards followed.

The English soldiers abandoned the forts, and the squadron sailed away the same day, carrying a hundred cannon and other military stores.

VI.—CAPTAIN PAUL JONES.

A short time after this, the American squadron tried to capture a British ship called the *Glasgow.* The attempt was not successful.

Because of this failure, one of the captains was dismissed from the navy, and the command of his vessel was given to Lieutenant Jones. This vessel was named the *Providence.*

With it and the *Alfred*, which he also commanded, Captain Jones captured sixteen prizes in
six weeks.   Among them were cargoes of coal and
dry goods.

Best of all, he captured an English vessel bound
for Canada, full of warm clothing for the British
soldiers.   This was a prize that proved of great
value to General Washington's poorly clothed
army.

In those days there were selfish people just as
now.   In January, 1777, a jealous commodore
succeeded in depriving Paul Jones of his position
as captain.   He was now without ship or rank.
When he appealed to Congress he was put off with
promises from time to time.   It was not until May
that his petitions were heard.

There were three new ships being built for the
navy at Boston.   Congress gave him permission
to choose one of these and have it fitted out as he
wished.

While waiting in Boston for these ships to be
finished, Paul Jones wrote many wise suggestions
about the management of the navy.   Congress at

first paid but little attention to these suggestions, but was afterwards glad to act upon them.

These were some of the things he said:

" 1. Every officer should be examined before he receives his commission.

BENJAMIN FRANKLIN.

" 2. The ranks in a navy should correspond to those in an army.

" 3. As England has the best navy in the world, we should copy hers."

Before the ship he had chosen was completed, he was ordered to wait no longer in Boston, but to take the *Ranger*, an old vessel, and sail at once for France. Through the efforts of Benjamin Franklin, the American Minister to France, the French king had acknowledged the independence of the colonies, and was ready to aid the Americans in the war.

Paul Jones was to carry a letter from Congress to the American commissioners in Paris.

This letter told the commissioners to buy a new fast-sailing frigate for Captain Jones, and to have it fitted up as he desired. They were then to advise him as to what he should do with it.

VII.—THE CRUISE OF THE RANGER.

When the *Ranger* sailed out of Boston harbor, the stars and stripes of the American republic waved from the mast head.

Paul Jones was the first naval officer to raise this flag. You remember that two years before, on the *Alfred*, he had first hoisted the pine tree emblem.

When he reached Quiberon Bay, in France, the admiral of the French fleet there saluted the American flag. This was the first time that a foreign country had recognized America as an independent nation.

Paul Jones anchored the *Ranger* at Brest and went to Paris to deliver his letter, and lay his plans before the commissioners. He told them two important things:

First, that our navy was too small to win in open battle with the fleets of the English.

Second, that the way to keep the English vessels from burning, destroying, and carrying away property on the American coasts, was to send vessels to the English coasts to annoy the English in the same way.

The commissioners thought that these plans should be carried out at once; and since a new frigate could not be purchased for some time, they refitted the *Ranger* for his use.

On April 10, 1778, Paul Jones set out on what proved to be a memorable cruise.

You remember that when he first went to sea, as a boy, he sailed from Whitehaven. This town is on the English coast, just across the Solway Firth from John Paul's old home.

He knew there were large shipping yards there, and he determined to set fire to them. He planned to reach the harbor in the night, and burn the ships while the people were asleep.

Because of the wind and tides, it was nearly midnight when he arrived. He found three hundred vessels of different kinds lying in the harbor. His men were put into two small boats, and each boat was ordered tc set fire to half the ships.

It was nearly daylight when they rowed away from the *Ranger*. Nothing could be heard but the splashing of their oars. Their flickering torches showed to them the old sleeping town, with the many white ships along the shore.

Leaving orders that the fire be speedily kindled, Captain Jones took with him a few men, and scaled the walls of the batteries which protected the harbor. He locked the sleeping sentinels in the guardhouse and spiked the cannon.

Then, sending his men back to the harbor, he went, with one man only, to another fort, which was a quarter of a mile away. Here he also spiked the guns.

After all this had been done he returned to his boats to find that his sailors had done nothing. Not one ship was on fire!

The lieutenant in charge told Paul Jones that their torches had gone out. "Anyway," he said, "nothing can be gained by burning poor people's property."

Determined that they should not leave the harbor until something was destroyed, Paul Jones ran to a neighboring house and got a light. With this he set fire to the largest ship.

By this time the people had been aroused, and hundreds were running to the shore.

There was no time to do more. The sailors hastened back to the *Ranger*, taking with them three prisoners, whom Paul Jones said he would show as "samples."

The soldiers tried to shoot the sailors from the forts; but they could do nothing with the spiked guns. The sailors amused themselves by firing back pistol shots.

On reaching the ship they found that a man was missing. Paul Jones was afraid that harm had befallen him. He need not have been troubled, however, for the man was a deserter. He spread the alarm for miles along the shore. The people afterward called him the "Savior of Whitehaven."

Paul Jones was greatly disappointed by the fail-

ure of his plans. He knew that if he had reached
the harbor a few hours earlier he could have
burned, not only all the ships, but the entire town.

Although the plan to destroy English property
to aid the American cause, was a wise one, from
a military point of view, yet we cannot understand
why Paul Jones should have selected Whitehaven
for this destruction. There he had received kindness and employment when a boy. His mother
and sisters lived just across the bay, and had he
succeeded in burning Whitehaven, the people, in
their anger, might have injured the family of the
man who had so cruelly harmed them. We won-
der if he thought of these things.

The Earl of Selkirk lived near Whitehaven, on
St. Mary's Isle. As the *Ranger* sailed by this
island, Paul Jones thought it would be well to take
the earl prisoner.

There were many Americans held as prisoners,
by the English, and the earl could be exchanged
for some of these.

So, with a few men, Paul Jones rowed to the
shore, where some fishermen told him that the earl

was away from home.   Paul Jones started to go
back to his vessel.   But his sailors were disappointed and asked his permission to go to the
earl's house and take away the silver.

Paul Jones did not like this plan, but at last consented. He did not go
with the men, how-
ever, but walked up
and down the shore
until they returned.

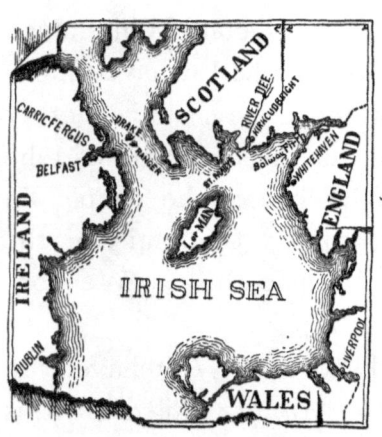

MAP OF THE IRISH SEA, SHOWING
THE CRUISE OF THE RANGER.

The sailors found
Lady Selkirk and her
family at breakfast.
They took all the sil-
ver from the table,
put it into a bag, and
returned to the ship.

Paul Jones was al-
ways troubled about this.   He afterwards bought
the silver for a large sum of money, and sent it
back to Lady Selkirk with a letter of apology.

The people in the neighborhood were frightened
when they heard of the earl's silver being taken.

They ran here and there, hiding their valuables. Some of them dragged a cannon to the shore, and spent a night firing at what they supposed in the darkness to be Paul Jones' vessel. In the morning they found they had wasted all their powder on a rock!

The next day the alarm was carried to all the towns along the shore: "Beware of Paul Jones, the pirate!"

VIII.—THE RANGER AND THE DRAKE.

An English naval vessel called the *Drake* was sent out to capture the *Ranger*. Every one felt sure that she would be successful, and five boat-loads of men went out with her to see the fight.

When the *Drake* came alongside of the *Ranger*, she hailed and asked what ship it was. Paul Jones replied: "The American Continental ship *Ranger!* Come on! We are waiting for you!"

After a battle of one hour, the *Drake* surrendered. The captain and forty-two men had been killed, and the vessel was badly injured. Paul

Jones lost only his lieutenant and one seaman.
Six others were wounded, one of whom died.

This was a great victory for Paul Jones. The
Drake not only mounted two more guns than the

THE "RANGER" AND THE "DRAKE."

Ranger, but was manned by a crew that was much
better drilled. The vessel belonged to the well-
established English navy, which was accustomed
to victory on the seas.

Towing the *Drake*, Paul Jones sailed northward in safety. Then, leaving the Irish Sea, he sailed around the north coast of Ireland and returned to the harbor at Brest, with the *Drake* and two hundred prisoners. This was just a month from the day he had set out on his cruise.

The French government had now concluded an alliance with the American republic. War had been openly declared between France and England, and all the French people rejoiced over the victory of the *Ranger*.

Paul Jones was not sorry when Congress sent him an order to bring his vessel to America. It was needed to protect the coasts of New Jersey from the war ships of the British.

The French king did not like brave Paul Jones to return to America. He wished him to remain where he could be of more direct service to France. He therefore caused letters to be sent to him, promising that if he would stay on that side of the Atlantic he should have command of the new frigate he had wished for so long.

Pleased with the prospect of this, he gave up

the command of the *Ranger*, and it sailed to America under a new captain.

But promises are often more easily made than kept. The French navy was well supplied with ships and officers. These officers were jealous of the success of Paul Jones, and did all they could to prevent him from obtaining his commission.

The summer and most of the winter of 1778 passed away, and Paul Jones was still waiting for his ship. He began to wish he had gone to America.

Some wealthy men offered him a ship if he would take charge of a trading expedition for them. To do this, he must give up his commission in the American navy, and so Paul Jones said, "As a servant of the republic of America, I cannot serve either myself or my best friends, unless the honor of America is the first object."

During these months of waiting, his only weapon was his pen. He wrote letters of appeal to all persons of influence, to Congress, and also to the king of France.

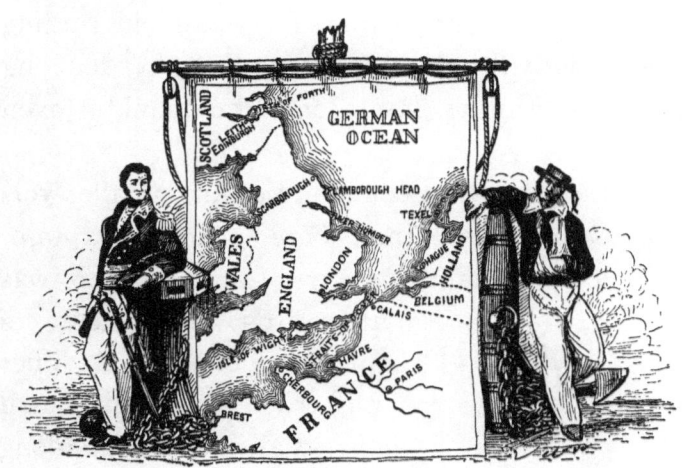

X.—The Bon Homme Richard. I

One day, when Paul Jones was reading "Poor Richard's Almanac," written by Dr. Franklin, he found a paragraph which set him to thinking. It was: *"If you would have your business done, go; if not,* SEND."

He sent no more letters, but went at once to the French court and pleaded his case there in person. As a result, he was soon after made commander of a vessel which he named the *Bon Homme Richard*, which means *Poor Richard*. He did this out of gratitude to Dr. Franklin.

The *Bon Homme Richard* was an old trading
vessel, poorly fitted out for war. But after his long
months of waiting, Paul Jones was thankful even
for this.

He was also given command of four smaller vessels. One of these, the *Alliance*, had, for captain,
a Frenchman named Pierre Landais, who was

afterwards the cause of
much trouble. Paul Jones
was ordered to cruise with
his small squadron along
the west coast of Ireland
and to capture all the English merchant vessels he
could find.

The officer next in com-
mand to Paul Jones was
Lieutenant Richard Dale,

RICHARD DALE.

who has since been remembered not only for his
bravery during that famous cruise, but for his service to the country at a later period.

On the 14th of August, 1779, the ships put to
sea. When they reach ed the southern point of Ire-

land, one of the four small vessels was left behind
and deserted.

Cruising northward, the squadron soon captured two valuable prizes. Without asking the
permission of Paul Jones, Captain Landais sent
these captured vessels to Norway.

On the way, they were taken by the Danes, who
returned them to England. The value of these
prizes, thus lost through Captain Landais, was
about £40,000, or nearly $200,000.

The squadron sailed round the north of Scotland, and down the eastern coast until it came to
the Firth of Forth. Here was the town of Leith,
and in its harbor lay some English war vessels.

Paul Jones wished to capture these. The winds
were favorable, and a landing could easily have
been made but for Captain Landais.

Paul Jones spent a whole night persuading
this troublesome captain to help him. It was
only with a promise of money that he at last
succeeded. But in the morning the winds were
contrary.

That day the *Richard* captured an English

merchant ship.   The captain promised Paul Jones that if he would allow his vessel to go free, he would pilot the squadron into the harbor.

The people, seeing the fleet piloted by the English vessel, supposed the visit to be a friendly one.   So they sent a boat out to the *Richard*, asking for powder and shot to defend the town from the visit of "Paul Jones the pirate."

Jones sent back a barrel of powder with the message that he had no suitable shot.   It was not until the vessels were nearing the harbor that the object of the visit was suspected.   The people, in their fright, ran to the house of the minister.   He had helped them when in trouble at other times, and could surely do something now.

The good man, with his flock following him, ran to the beach, where he made a strange prayer.

He told the Lord that the people there were very poor, and that the wind was bringing to the shore that "vile pirate," Paul Jones, who would burn their houses and take away even their clothes. "I canna think of it!   I canna think of it!   I have long been a faithful servant to ye, O Lord.

But gin ye dinna turn the wind aboot and blaw the scoundrel out of our gates, I'll nae stir a foot, but will just sit here till the tide comes in."

Just then a violent gale sprang up, and by the time it had abated the squadron had been driven so far out to sea that the plan was given up.

Long afterward, the good minister would often say, "I prayed, but the Lord sent the wind."

X.—THE GREAT FIGHT WITH THE SERAPIS.

Paul Jones next cruised up and down the eastern coast of England, trying to capture some merchant ships that were bound for London.

About noon, on September 23, 1779, he saw not far from the shore an English fleet, sailing from the north. It was convoyed by two new war ships, the *Serapis* and the *Countess of Scarborough*.

Paul Jones at once signaled to his ships to form in line of battle. Captain Landais disobeyed.

The sight of the American squadron seemed to cause confusion in the English fleet. They let fly their top gallant sails and fired many signals.   The *Serapis* and the *Countess* drew up in line of battle and waited for the enemy, while the merchant ships ran into port.

It was a clear, calm afternoon.   The sea was like a polished mirror, with scarcely a ripple on its surface.

The vessels approached each other so slowly that they scarcely seemed to move.   The decks had all been cleared for action, and the captains were full of impatience.

Word had gone from town to town along the shore, that a great battle was soon to be fought. The people along the shore gathered on the high cliffs, eagerly hoping to see the dreaded Paul Jones crushed forever.

The sun had gone down behind the hills before the ships were within speaking distance of each other.   The harvest moon came up, full and clear, and shed a soft light over the dreadful battle that followed.

Captain Landais, when he disobeyed Paul Jones' order to join in line of battle, spread the sails of the *Alliance*, and went quickly toward the enemy as though to make an attack. But when very near to where the *Serapis* lay, he changed his course, and sailed away to a place where the battle could be seen without harm.

About half-past seven in the evening, the *Richard* rounded to on the side of the *Serapis* within pistol-shot.

Captain Pearson of the *Serapis* hailed, saying: "What ship is that?" The answer came: "I can't hear what you say."

Captain Pearson repeated: "What ship is that? Answer at once or I shall fire."

Paul Jones' reply was a shot. This was followed by a broadside from each vessel.

At this first fire, two of the guns in the lower battery of the *Richard* burst. The explosion tore up the decks, and killed many men.

The two vessels now began pouring broadsides into each other. The *Richard* was old and rotten, and these shots caused her to leak badly. Captain Pearson saw this, and hailed, saying, "Has your ship struck?"

The bold reply came: "I have not yet begun to fight."

Paul Jones saw, that, as the *Serapis* was so much the better ship of the two, his only hope lay in getting the vessels so close together that the men could board the *Serapis* from the *Richard*.

All this time the vessels had been sailing in the same direction, crossing and re-crossing each other's course.

Finally Paul Jones ran the *Richard* across the bow of the *Serapis*. The anchor of the *Serapis* caught in the stern of the *Richard* and became firmly fastened there. As the vessels were swung around by the tide, the sides came together. The spars and rigging were entangled and remained so until the close of the engagement.

With the muzzles of the guns almost touching, the firing began. The effect was terrible.

Paul Jones, who had only two guns that could be used on the starboard side, grappled with the *Serapis*. With the help of a few men, he brought over a larboard gun, and these three were all that he used during the rest of the battle.

Meanwhile the other ships of the American squadron did strange things. The *Pallas*, alone, did her duty. In a half hour she had captured the *Countess of Scarborough.* The *Vengeance* simply sailed for the nearest harbor.

Worst of all was the conduct of Captain Landais and his ship *Alliance.* For a while he looked quietly on as though he were umpire. At 9:30 o'clock he came along the larboard side of the *Richard* so that she was between him and the enemy. Then he deliberately fired into her, killing many men.

Many voices cried out that he was firing into the wrong ship. He seemed not to hear, for, until the battle was over, his firing continued. The *Poor Richard* had an enemy on each side.

Paul Jones sent some men up the masts and into the rigging to throw hand-grenades, or bombs, among the enemy. One of these set fire to some cartridges on the deck of the *Serapis.* This caused a terrible explosion, disabling all the men at the guns in that part of the ship. Twenty of them were killed outright.

By this time so much water had leaked into the *Richard* that she was settling. A sailor, seeing this, set up the cry: "Quarter! quarter! Our ship is sinking!"

Captain Pearson, hearing the cry, sent his men to board the *Richard*. Paul Jones, with a pike in his hand, headed a party of his men similarly armed, and drove the English back.

Some of the *Richard's* men ran below and set the prisoners free. There were more than a hundred of them.

One of these prisoners climbed through the port holes into the *Serapis*. He told Captain Pearson that if he would hold out a little longer, the *Richard* would either sink or strike.

Poor Paul Jones was now in a hard place. His ship was sinking. More than a hundred prisoners were running about the decks, and they, with the crew, were shouting for quarter. His own ship, the *Alliance*, was hurling shots at him from the other side. Everywhere was confusion.

But he, alone, was undismayed. He shouted to the prisoners to go below to the pumps or they would be quickly drowned. He ordered the crew to their places. He himself never left the three guns that could still be fired.

At half-past ten o'clock, the *Serapis* surrendered.

When Captain Pearson gave his sword to Paul

THE "SERAPIS" AND THE "BON HOMME RICHARD."

Jones, he said it was very hard to surrender to a man who had fought "with a halter around his neck." Paul Jones replied, "Sir! You have fought like a hero. I hope your king will reward you."

This battle had lasted for three hours and a half.

It has since been known in history as one of the greatest victories ever won upon the seas. The *Serapis* and the *Countess* were both new ships, one of forty guns and the other of twenty. The crews were well-drilled Englishmen.

Everything was against the *Richard*, and the victory was due alone to the great courage and will of its commander. When the fight was over, Paul Jones separated the ships and set the sails of the *Richard*. All night every sailor was busy fighting the fire which raged on both ships.

When daylight showed to Captain Pearson the wreck of the *Richard*, he was sorry he had surrendered. Her rudder was gone and her rotten timbers were split into pieces. Some of the shots had passed entirely through her.

Paul Jones wished to take her into port to show how desperately he had fought, but this was out of the question. By nine o'clock the sailors abandoned her, and at ten she suddenly went down.

Repairing the *Serapis* as best he could, Paul Jones took her and the *Countess of Scarborough*, with his unfaithful fleet, to Holland.

XI.—HONOR TO THE HERO.

After this great victory, Paul Jones was everywhere received as a hero. The king of France presented him with a gold sword.

He also sent word, through his minister, that, with the consent of Congress, he would make Paul Jones a Knight of the Order of Military Merit. To avoid delay, the gold cross of the order had been sent to the French minister in America, who would present it to Paul Jones when permission to accept it had been received from Congress.

The hero traveled about in Holland and France, from city to city, enjoying his great triumph. Crowds of people were everywhere eager to see him, and a word with him was thought to be a great honor.

The most serious fault in the character of Paul Jones was his vanity. He had always been very fond of praise and glory, and now his longings were partly satisfied by all this homage.

Dr. Franklin wrote him a letter, praising him for his bravery. He thanked him, most of all, for the prisoners he had captured. There were so many of them that, by exchange, every American, held by the English, could be set at liberty.

While Paul Jones was enjoying this praise, Captain Landais was going about also, claiming for himself the glory for the capture of the *Serapis*, and trying to make people believe that he was the real hero.

When Dr. Franklin heard from the sailors how he had fired upon the *Richard*, he ordered him to Paris to be tried.

During the next year, Paul Jones made a few short cruises, but accomplished nothing more than the taking of a few prizes.

At this time the army of George Washington was sorely in need of clothing **and** military supplies. Word was sent to Dr. Franklin to buy them in France and send them to America by Paul Jones.

Fifteen thousand muskets, with powder, and one hundred and twenty bales of cloth, were bought and stored in the *Alliance* and the *Ariel*. Dr. Franklin told Paul Jones to sail with these goods at once. This was early in the year 1780.

The summer came and passed away, and the ships were still anchored in the French harbor. Paul Jones gave excuse after excuse until the patience of Dr. Franklin was about gone.

Captain Landais had been one cause of the delay. Instead of going to Paris for trial, as Franklin had ordered, he had gone back to the *Alliance* to stir up mutiny against Paul Jones. He caused one trouble after another and disobeyed every order. Finally, by intrigue, he took command of the *Alliance* and sailed to America.

But Captain Landais never again troubled Paul Jones. His reception in America was not what he had expected. Instead of being regarded as a hero, he was judged insane, and dismissed from the navy. A small share of prize money was afterward paid to him. On this he lived until eighty-seven years of age, when he died in Brooklyn, New York.

Another reason Paul Jones gave for his delay in France was that he wished to get the prize money due for the capture of the *Serapis*, and pay the sailors. This gave him an excuse to

linger about the courts where he could receive
more of the homage he loved so well.

Then, too, he spent much time in getting letters and certificates of his bravery from the king
and the ministers. He wished to show these to
Congress when he should arrive in America.

Finally, one day in October, he set sail in the
Ariel. He had not gone far when a furious gale
forced him to return to port for safety.

For three months longer he waited, hoping still
for the prize money that was due. One day he
gave a grand fête on his ship. Flags floated from
every mast. Pink silk curtains hung from awn-
ings to the decks. These were decorated with
mirrors, pictures, and flowers.

The company invited were men and women of
high rank. When all was ready, Paul Jones sent
his boats ashore to bring them on board.

He, himself, dressed in full uniform, received
them and conducted them to their seats on the
deck. At three o'clock they sat down to an
elaborate dinner which lasted until sunset.

At eight o'clock, as the moon rose, a mock

battle of the *Richard* and the *Serapis* was given.
There was much noise from the firing of guns,
and a great blaze of light from the rockets that
were sent up. The effect was beautiful, but the
din was such that the ladies were frightened. At
the end of an hour this display was ende d.

After a dance on the deck, the officers rowed
the company back to the shore.

XII.—The Return to America.

On the 18th of December, 1780, nearly a year
after he had received his orders, Jones sailed for
America. He arrived in Philadelphia on February 18th, 1781. When Congress inquired into
the cause of his long delay, he gave explanations
which seemed to be satisfactory. Resolutions of
thanks were passed, and permission given to the
French minister to present the Cross of Military
Merit, which had been sent by the French king.

This cross was presented with great ceremony,
and it was ever after a source of much pride to

Paul Jones.   He wore it upon all occasions and
loved to be called Chevalier.

During the following year Paul Jones superin-
tended the construction of a new war ship, the
America, which was being built by Congress.

This was the largest seventy-four gun ship in
the world, and he was to be her captain.

Once more Paul Jones was disappointed. Before the *America* was finished, Congress decided
to give her to France.   She was to replace a
French vessel, which had been lost while in the
American service.

Paul Jones was again without a ship.   As he
could not bear to be idle, he spent the time until
the close of the war, with a French fleet, cruising among the West Indies.

As soon as he heard that peace was declared
between England and America, he left the French
fleet and returned to America.   He arrived in
Philadelphia in May, 1783.

Now that the war was over, and there was no
more fighting to be done, Paul Jones thought
that the best thing for him to do was to get the

prize money still due from the French government for the vessels he had captured.

For this purpose, he soon returned to France.
After many delays the money, amounting to nearly
$30,000, was paid to him. It was to be divided
among the officers and crews of the ships which
he had commanded.

Paul Jones came again to America in 1787 to
attend to the final division of this money.

While in this country, Congress ordered a gold
medal to be presented to him for his services during the war.

XIII.—Ambitious Hopes.

You remember that, during the war, Captain
Landais had sent two valuable ships to Norway,
and so caused the loss of much prize money.

Denmark had taken these ships, by force, and given them back to England.

Paul Jones determined to go to Denmark to try to induce that country to pay for these ships. In November, 1787, he left America for the last time.

On the way to Denmark, he stopped in Paris. Here he heard some news which pleased him very much.

For some time Russia had been at war with Turkey, and the Russian navy had lately met with several disasters on the Black Sea.

The Russian minister in Paris had heard a great deal about the hero, Paul Jones. So he sent word to the Empress Catherine, who was then the ruler of Russia, that if she would give Paul Jones the command of the Russian fleet, ''all Constantinople would tremble in less than a year.''

When Paul Jones heard that this message had gone to Russia, he was sure that a chance would come to win still more glory and fame.

He was more anxious than before to go to Copenhagen, the capital of Denmark. He would then be nearer to Russia and could more quickly answer the summons of the empress.

He was not disappointed in this. He was in Copenhagen but a few weeks, when he received the offer of a position in the Russian navy, with the rank of rear-admiral.

He gave up the hope of the prize money, and started in April, 1788, for St. Petersburg.

The story of his trip to Russia shows what a fearless man he was. No danger was too great for him to brave, in order to accomplish any purpose he had in mind.

In order to reach St. Petersburg with the least delay, he went to Stockholm, Sweden. Here he took an open boat and crossed the Baltic Sea, which was full of floating ice.

He did not let the boatmen know of his intentions until they were well out at sea. Then, pistol in hand, he compelled the unwilling men to steer for the Russian shore.

For four days and nights they were out in the open boats, carefully steering through the ice, and many times barely escaping death.

When, at last, they arrived safely at a Russian port on the Gulf of Finland, he rewarded the boatmen and gave them a new boat and provisions for their return. Scarcely would any one believe the story, as such a trip had never been made before, and was thought to be impossible.

He hurried on to St. Petersburg, where he was warmly welcomed. The story of his trip across the Baltic, added to other tales of his bravery, caused the empress to show him many favors.

XIV.—SAD DISAPPOINTMENTS.

After a few days in St. Petersburg, Paul Jones hurried on to the Black Sea to take command of his fleet. But he again met with disappointments. He was not given the command of the whole fleet, as he had expected. Instead, he was given only half, Prince Nassau commanding the remainder. Both of these men were under a still higher authority, Prince Potemkin.

Potemkin was as fond of glory as was Paul

Jones. He and Nassau were both jealous of the
foreigner, and Potemkin finally succeeded in
having Paul Jones recalled to St. Petersburg.

He arrived there, full of sorrow, because he had
achieved no fame. More trouble was in store for
him. Some jealous conspirators so blackened
his character that the empress would not allow
him to appear at court.

Even after proving his innocence to the satisfac-
tion of the empress, he could not regain his
former position.

About this time his health began to fail. Sick,
both in body and mind, he went back to Paris in
1790, having been in Russia about eighteen
months.

It was nearly a year afterward, before he gave
up all hope of regaining a position in the Russian
service. When the empress refused him this, he
quietly waited for death.

This occurred on the 18th of July, 1792, in his
lodgings in Paris. His pride and love of titles had
left him. He told his friends that he wished no
longer to be called Admiral or Chevalier.

He wished to be simply a "citizen of the United States."

The National Assembly of France decreed him a public funeral, and many of the greatest men of the time followed his body to the tomb. The place of his burial has been forgotten.

The most enduring monument to his memory is to be found in the grateful recollections of his countrymen. The name of Paul Jones, the first naval hero of America, will not be forgotten so long as the stars and stripes float over the sea.

THE STORY OF

OLIVER HAZARD PERRY

O. H. Perry

THE STORY OF OLIVER HAZARD PERRY

I.—How the Perry Family Came to Rhode Island.

A very long time ago, there lived in England a young Quaker whose name was Edmund Perry.

At that time the Quakers were much persecuted. They were a quiet and peace-loving people, and would not serve in the army. They had their own religious meetings, and refused to pay money for the support of the Church of England. For these reasons, they were imprisoned, beaten, and driven from their homes.

Edmund Perry believed that the Quakers were right, and he could not endure these persecutions. So, in 1650, he came to America to live.

Thirty years before that time, a company of Pilgrims had left England because they also wished to be free to worship God as they chose.

They had founded a colony at Plymouth, which is now in the state of Massachusetts.

Edmund Perry thought that in this settlement of Pilgrims he could surely live peaceably in the enjoyment of his own belief. He did not stay long in Plymouth, however. His Quaker religion was hated there, as it had been in England; and the Pilgrims did not wish to have any one in their colony who did not agree with them.

Not far from Plymouth was the colony of Rhode Island, which had been founded by Roger Williams. Roger Williams declared that a man is responsible for his opinions only to God and his own conscience, and that no one has any right to punish him for his belief.

The people in the Rhode Island colony did not quarrel with one another about religion, but lived together in peace.

Edmund Perry thought that this was the place where he could make a home for himself and his family. He therefore purchased a large tract of land on the shores of Narragansett Bay, near what is now the site of South Kingston.

Here he lived for the rest of his life, at peace
with all about him, even his Indian neighbors.
His descendants also lived in this neighborhood.
Among them were judges, lawyers, and doctors, as
well as farmers and mechanics; and they were
always highly respected in the colony.

Christopher Raymond Perry, a great-great-
grandson of Edmund Perry, was born in December, 1761.

At that time there were thirteen colonies or
great settlements of English people at different
places along the Atlantic coast of what is now the
United States. But troubles had already begun
to brew between the people of these colonies and
the king of England. These troubles finally led
to the Revolutionary War.

Christopher Perry, although a mere boy, was
one of the first persons in Rhode Island to offer
himself for this war. He joined a company of volunteers known as the "Kingston Reds"; but soon
afterwards left the army and entered the navy.
Here he served, having many adventures, until
the close of the war, in 1783.

He had become very fond of a sailor's life, and when there was no more use for him in the navy he obtained a place on a merchant vessel, and went on a cruise to Ireland.

During the homeward voyage he became acquainted with one of the passengers, a beautiful girl of Scotch descent, whose name was Sara Alexander. Soon after their arrival in America, their friendship ripened into love, and in 1784 they were married in Philadelphia.

Christopher Perry, though but twenty-three years of age, was then the captain of a vessel. The young couple went to live with Christopher's father, on the old Perry estate in South Kingston.

This was then a farm of two hundred acres. The old homestead stood at the foot of a hill not far from the Narragansett shore.

Through the trees in a neighboring wood, shone the white stones which marked the graves of the Quaker, Edmund Perry, and many of his children and grandchildren.

The Perry family were glad to welcome Christopher's young wife into their home. She was as intelligent as she was beautiful ; and her sweet and happy disposition made every one love her.

Christopher Perry gave up his life on the sea for a time, and many happy months were spent in the old home.

On the 23d of August, 1785, their first baby boy was born.   He was named for an uncle and a great-great-grandfather, Oliver Hazard Perry.

II.—School Days.

Oliver was a winsome baby and he grew strong and beautiful very fast.   Every one loved him, for he thought all strangers were friends, and was never afraid of them.

Indeed he was not afraid of anything, for to him there was no danger.   We shall see that he kept this same fearlessness all through his life.

When he was three years old, he was playing one day with an older child, in the road near his grandfather's house.   A man was seen coming rapidly towards them on horseback.   The elder child ran out of the way, calling to Oliver to do the same.

The little fellow sat quite still, however, until the horse was nearly upon him.   As the horseman

CHILDHOOD HOME OF OLIVER PERRY.

drew rein, Oliver looked up into his face and said, " Man, you will not ride over me, will you? "

The gentleman, who was a friend of the family's, carried him into the house, and told the story.

When scarcely more than a baby, Oliver sat

upon his mother's knee, while she taught him letters and words. It was not long before he could read quite well. By the time he was five years old, there were two other babies to keep the beautiful, loving mother busy. So it was thought best to send Oliver to school.

Not far from the Perrys', there lived an old gentleman whom the people loved because of his goodness of heart. As there was no school near by, he had often been asked to teach the neighborhood children.

The good old man was notoriously lazy, and consented upon one condition—that he should be allowed to have a bed in the schoolroom.

Teachers were few in those days, and, since there was no one else, the bed was set up. How amusing it must have been to see the children standing about the master's bed and reciting their lessons!

It was to this strange school that little Oliver was first sent. Some girl cousins lived on the adjoining farm. Though they were all older than he, it was Oliver's duty, each day, to take them to

and from school.   No one, not even the other
scholars, thought this at all strange.   His dignified
manners always made him seem older than he
really was.

One day his mother told him that he was old
enough to go to school at Tower Hill, a place four
miles away.   Boys and girls would now think that
a long way to go to school ; but Oliver and his
cousins did not mind the walk through the woods
and over the hills.

The master of this school was so old that he had
once taught Oliver's grandfather.   He was not lazy,
however, and was never known to lose his temper.

It was not long until a change was made and
Oliver was taken away from "old master Kelly."

For several years past, Oliver's father had been
again on the sea.   He had commanded vessels on
successful voyages to Europe and South America,
and now he had a large income.   He was therefore able to pay for better teaching for Oliver and
the younger children.

So the family moved from South Kingston to
Newport, a larger town, with better schools.

At first Oliver did not like the change. The discipline was much more strict than it had been in the little country schools.

His teacher, Mr. Frazer, had one serious fault. He had a violent temper which was not always controlled.

One day he became angry at Oliver and broke a ruler over his head. Without a word, Oliver took his hat and went home. He told his mother that he would never go back.

The wise mother said nothing until the next morning. Then, giving him a note for Mr. Frazer, she told him to go to school as usual. The proud boy's lip quivered and tears were in his eyes, but he never thought of disobeying his mother.

The note he carried was a kind one, telling Mr. Frazer that she intrusted Oliver to his care again and hoped that she would not have cause to regret it.

After this Oliver had no better friend than Mr. Frazer. On holidays they walked together to the seashore and spent many hours wandering along

the beach.   The schoolmaster took great delight in
teaching Oliver the rules of navigation, and the use
of the instruments necessary for sailing a vessel.

Oliver learned these things so readily that it
was not long until Mr. Frazer said he was the best
navigator in Rhode Island.   This, of course, was
not strictly true, but it showed what an apt scholar
the boy was.

Oliver made many friends in Newport.   Among
them was the Frenchman, Count Rochambeau.
The father of this man was a great general, and
had once commanded some French troops who
helped the Americans in the Revolutionary War.

Count Rochambeau often invited Oliver to dine
with him, and one day he gave him a beautiful
little watch.

When Oliver was twelve years old, his father
gave up his life on the sea.   The family then
moved to Westerly, a little village in the southwestern part of Rhode Island.

For five years Oliver had been a faithful pupil
of Mr. Frazer's, and he was now far advanced
for his years.

III.—PLANS FOR THE FUTURE.

About this time some unexpected troubles arose in our country.

France and England had been at war for years. The French were anxious that America should join in the quarrel; and when they could not bring this about by persuasion, they tried to use force.

French cruisers were sent to the American shores to capture merchant vessels while on their way to foreign ports.

You may be sure that this roused the people from one end of the United States to the other. Preparations for war with France were begun; and the first great need was a better navy.

At the close of the Revolutionary War, all work on government vessels had been stopped. Those that were unfinished were sold to shipping merchants. Even the ships of war that had done such good service, were sold to foreign countries. In this way, the entire American navy passed out of existence.

But now the President, John Adams, went to work to establish a navy that should give protection to American commerce.

In the spring of 1798, a naval department was organized, with Benjamin Stoddart as the first Secretary of the Navy. The following summer was busy with active preparations. Six new frigates were built, and to these were added a number of other vessels of various kinds.

Captain Christopher Perry was given command of one of the new frigates that were being built at Warren, a small town near Bristol, Rhode Island. This vessel was to be called the *General Greene.*

In order to superintend the building of this vessel, Captain Perry, with his wife, left his quiet home in Westerly, and went to stay in Warren.

Oliver, then not quite thirteen years old, remained at home to take charge of the family.

He saw that his sister and brothers went to school regularly. He bought all the family provisions. Each day he wrote to his father and mother, telling them about home affairs. In the meantime, he was busily planning what his work in life should be.

His mother had taught him that a man must be brave, and always ready to serve his country. She had told him many stories of battles fought long ago in her native land across the sea.

Oliver had lived most of his life in sight of the sea, and had spent many hours with seamen. It is not strange, therefore, that he should decide,—" I wish to be a captain like my father."

He had heard of the troubles with France, and he longed to help defend his country. And so at last he wrote to his father, asking permission to enter the navy. It was a manly letter, telling all his reasons for his choice.

The consent was readily given, and Oliver soon afterward received an appointment as midshipman on his father's vessel, the *General Greene*.

IV.—THE CRUISE IN THE WEST INDIES.

In the meantime, the people grew more eager for war. An army had been raised to drive back

the French, should they attempt to invade the
land.   George Washington, though nearly sixty-
seven years of age, had been appointed commander in chief of the American forces.

In February, 1799, one
of the new frigates, the *Constellation*, under Captain
Truxton, defeated and captured a French frigate of
equal size.   By spring the
General Greene was com-
pleted, and Captain Perry
was ordered to sail for the
West Indies.

CAPT. THOMAS TRUXTON.

America had large trad-
ing interests with those islands.   Many of our
merchant vessels brought from there large cargoes
of fruits, coffee, and spices.   The *General Greene*
was ordered to protect these cargoes from the
French cruisers, and bring them safely into port.

For several months Captain Perry's vessel convoyed ships between Cuba and the United States.
In July, some of the sailors on board were sick

with yellow fever.   So Captain Perry brought the
vessel back to Newport.

Oliver went at once to see his mother.   The
tall lad in his bright uniform was a hero to all
the children in the neighborhood.

His brothers and sister considered it an honor to
wait upon him.   They would go out in the early
morning and pick berries for his breakfast, so that
he might have them with the dew upon them.

While on shipboard he had learned to play a
little on the flute.   The children loved to sit about
him, and listen to his music.

By the autumn of 1799, the crew of the *General
Greene* were well again, and Captain Perry sailed
back to Havana.

It was during the following winter months of
cruising with his father, that Oliver was taught his
lessons of naval honor.   He also applied the
lessons in navigation which he had learned from
Mr. Frazer.

He read and studied very carefully, and could
not have had a better teacher than his father.

While the *General Greene* was cruising among

the West Indies, Captain Truxton had won
another victory with his *Constellation.* This time
he captured a French frigate which carried sixteen
guns more than the *Constellation.*

The French, dismayed at these victories of the
Americans, began to be more civil. They even
seemed anxious for peace.

THE CONSTELLATION.

War had been carried on for about a year,
though it had never been formally declared.

In May, 1800, the *General Greene* came back to
Newport, and remained in harbor until the terms
of peace were concluded.

The trouble with France being settled, it was

decided by the government to dispose of nearly all the naval vessels. As a result, many of the captains and midshipmen were dismissed, Captain Perry being one of the number.

Fortunately for the country, young Oliver was retained as midshipman.

V.—THE WAR WITH THE BARBARY STATES.

On the northern coast of Africa, bordering on the Mediterranean Sea, are four countries known as the Barbary States. These are Tunis, Algiers, Tripoli, and Morocco.

For more than four hundred years, these countries had been making a business of sea-robbery. Their pirate vessels had seized and plundered the ships of other nations, and the captured officers and men were sold into slavery.

Instead of resisting these robbers, most of the nations had found it easier to pay vast sums of money to the Barbary rulers to obtain protection for their commerce.

The Americans had begun in this way, and had

made presents of money and goods to Algiers and Tunis.

Then the ruler of Tripoli, called the Bashaw, informed our government that he would wait six months for a handsome present from us.   If it did

not come then, he would declare war against the United States.

This did not frighten the Americans at all. Their only reply was to send a fleet of four vessels to the Mediterranean.   The intention was to force the Bashaw to make a treaty which should insure safety for our vessels.

COMMODORE CHARLES MORRIS.

This squadron did not do much but blockade the ports of Tripoli.

A year later, in 1802, a larger squadron was fitted out to bring the Bashaw to terms.   Commodore Morris was the commander.   On one of the vessels, the *Adams*, was Oliver Perry as midshipman.

Soon after the arrival of his ship in the Mediterranean, Oliver celebrated his seventeenth birthday.

The captain of the *Adams* was very fond of him, and succeeded in having him appointed lieutenant on that day.

For a year and a half, the squadron of Commodore Morris cruised about the Mediterranean. No great battles were fought and no great victories were won.

The *Adams* stopped at the coast towns of Spain, France, and Italy. Through the kindness of the captain, Oliver was often allowed to go on shore and visit the places of interest.

Commodore Morris, being recalled to America, sailed thither in the *Adams;* and so it happened that in November, 1803, Oliver Perry arrived again in America.

His father was then living in Newport, and Oliver remained at home until July of the next year.

He spent much of his time in studying mathematics and astronomy. He liked to go out among the young people, and his pleasing man-

ners and good looks made him a general fa-
vorite.

He was fond of music and could play the flute
very skillfully. When not studying, he liked most
of all to ride horses, and fence with a sword.

While Lieutenant Perry was spending this time
at home, the war in the Mediterranean was still
being carried on. Commodore Preble, who had
succeeded Commodore Morris, had won many
brilliant victories.

The most daring feat of all this war was accomplished by Stephen Decatur, a young lieutenant
only twenty-three years old.

One of the largest of the American vessels, the
Philadelphia, had, by accident, been grounded on
a reef. Taking advantage of her helpless condition,
the whole Tripolitan fleet opened fire upon her.

Captain Bainbridge, the commander of the
Philadelphia, was obliged to surrender. The
Tripolitans managed to float the vessel off the
reef, and towed her into the harbor.

Captain Bainbridge, although a prisoner, found
means to send word of his misfortune to Commo-

dore Preble, who was then at Malta, and the American fleet at once sailed for Tripoli.

At the suggestion of Captain Bainbridge, the Americans determined to burn the *Philadelphia*, rather than allow the Tripolitans to keep her.

This was a very dangerous undertaking, as the vessel was anchored in the midst of the Tripolitan fleet. It was also within easy range of the guns of the fort, commanding the harbor.

The task was given to Stephen Decatur. In order to deceive the enemy, he took a small boat which had been captured from them a short time before. Its crew was made up of volunteers, for the chances of escape were very few.

STEPHEN DECATUR.

Under cover of night, the little vessel sailed into the harbor, and, as if by accident, ran into the *Philadelphia*. Before the Tripolitans realized what had happened, Decatur and his men were climbing over the sides of the vessel and through the port holes.

Decatur had ordered his men to use no fire-arms. He did not wish to attract the attention of

BURNING OF THE PHILADELPHIA.

the Tripolitans who were in the fort and on the other vessels in the harbor.

A desperate hand to hand fight ensued. In a few minutes the Americans were in possession of the vessel. Some of the Tripolitan crew had been killed; others had jumped into the sea.

The Americans then set the *Philadelphia* on

fire and jumped into their boat to escape. Lieutenant Decatur was the last one to leave the burning ship.

The situation of the little band was now desperate. The *Philadelphia* was a mass of flames, lighting up the harbor for miles around.

Decatur's little boat could be plainly seen, and all the vessels and forts opened fire on it. But the Tripolitans were too much excited to do serious damage.

In a short time the fire reached the magazine of the *Philadelphia* and she blew up with a tremendous crash, leaving the harbor in darkness. Decatur and his men escaped with but one man wounded.

This is only one of many deeds of bravery done in this war, but we can not tell of them in this story. Lieutenant Perry, in his home in America, heard of them, and longed to be on the scene of action.

He was very glad when, in the following September, he was ordered to return in the *Constellation* to the Mediterranean.

The American fleet in the Mediterranean was by this time so large that the Bashaw was convinced that the Americans were in earnest.

He was glad to make a treaty of peace and release the prisoners on payment of a small ransom.

In October, 1806, Oliver Perry returned to America. He was greatly disappointed that he had not been able to take a more active part in the war.

He spent most of the next two years in Newport, dividing his time between study and his many friends.

VI.—MORE TROUBLE WITH ENGLAND.

While America was having these troubles with the Barbary States, France and England were still at war. Commerce all over the world was affected, and in some cases almost destroyed by this long war.

The French emperor, Napoleon Bonaparte, had forbidden all vessels of other nations to enter

British ports. The English, in turn, said that no vessel should enter a port of France, or of any country belonging to France.

But the Americans had to endure still further injuries from the English. British war vessels claimed the right to stop American ships on the sea, search them, and carry off American sailors, claiming them as deserters from the English navy.

The French could not do this ; for no American sailor could be accused of being a runaway Frenchman.

In 1807, an event took place which nearly led to war.

The British frigate *Leopard*, cruising along the coast, hailed the American frigate *Chesapeake*, and demanded permission to search the ship.

The captain of the *Chesapeake* refused. Without a word of warning, the *Leopard* fired into the *Chesapeake*, killing and wounding more than twenty men.

The American captain had not dreamed of such an outrage. His vessel had just put to sea and everything was in confusion. He did not even have a gun in condition to return the fire. So he lowered his flag and surrendered.

The officers of the *Leopard* then came on board and carried off four men from the crew.

The United States would have declared war at once if England had not apologized.

The President, at this time, was Thomas Jefferson. He was a man of peace. He called a session of Congress to see if the trouble could not be settled without war.

As a result of this session, a law was passed known as the Embargo Act. By this law, no vessel was allowed to sail from the United States to any foreign country.

In order to enforce the law, Congress ordered a number of gunboats to be built. These were to sail up and down the coast, and prevent any vessel from entering or leaving the ports.

Lieutenant Perry was ordered to superintend the building of a fleet of these gunboats at Newport. After they were built, he was put in command of them, and ordered to patrol Long Island Sound.

At this time, the government wanted a map of the harbors in the neighborhood of Newport. On account of his standing as a seaman, and of his education, Lieutenant Perry was selected to visit the harbors and make such a map.

He was given a fast sailing schooner called the *Revenge.* While carrying on this work, he was one day returning from Newport to New London, when a dense fog came on. The *Revenge* struck upon a reef of rocks, and went to pieces.

By great efforts Lieutenant Perry was able to save, not only all the crew, but the sails, rigging, and cannon.

He then went to Washington to explain the loss of the *Revenge* to the navy department. It was made clear that it was the fault of the local pilot who had charge of the vessel at the time.

Lieutenant Perry was commended for his gallant conduct in this disaster, and was also granted a year's leave of absence. He went to Newport, and on May 5, 1811, he was married to Elizabeth Champlin Mason.

The young couple took a wedding journey

through New England. They spent one day in Plymouth, Massachusetts. Lieutenant Perry was much interested in visiting the place where his Quaker ancestor had lived so many years before.

During this time, the people of the United States had learned that the Embargo Act was a very unwise law. The men of Congress had thought to injure France and England by thus refusing to trade with them altogether. They soon

discovered, however, that the damage to American commerce was far greater.

Trading vessels in the ports were left standing idle at the wharves, while the sailors were forced to find

JAMES MADISON.   other employment.

All over the country, there arose a bitter feeling against this law. In the New England states, where there were the largest shipping interests, there was even talk of secession from the Union.

About this time a new President, James Madison, was elected. Soon afterward the Embargo Act was repealed, and in its place was passed a law which satisfied the people for a time. By this law, trade was allowed with every country but England and France.

American vessels now put to sea on voyages to foreign lands. But their old enemies, the English, soon began to annoy them as before.

In May, 1811, the British sloop *Little Belt* was hailed by the American frigate *President*, under the command of Commodore Rodgers. The reply was a cannon shot. The *President* then poured broadsides into the *Little Belt*. After the

COMMODORE JOHN RODGERS.

English had lost thirty-two men in killed and wounded, they came to terms.

The American people now saw that war could no longer be avoided. On June 18, 1812, the formal declaration was made.

VII.—War on the Canadian Border.

Up to this time the English navy had been called the "Mistress of the Seas." England's vessels could be numbered by the hundred, and the crews by the ten thousand.

When this war of 1812 was declared, the entire United States navy comprised about half a dozen frigates, and six or eight sloops and brigs. Along the American coast alone the English had seven times this number of war vessels.

The first few months of the war were full of naval surprises. In that brief time the Americans captured more British ships than the French had taken in twenty years.

On August 19th, the American frigate *Constitution*, commanded by Captain Isaac Hull, in one half hour captured the English frigate *Guerrière*. The English lost one hundred men, and the vessel was so disabled that she was left to sink. The Americans lost but fourteen men, and in a few hours the ship was ready for another battle.

Several other victories followed in quick succes-

sion.   In all this time the Americans did not lose
a ship.

In December, Commodore Bainbridge, the same
officer who had been taken prisoner years before
by the Tripolitans and had afterwards been promoted, was cruising with the frigate *Constitution*
off the coast of Brazil.   He there encountered and
captured the British frigate *Java*.

But though so successful on the sea, the Americans were defeated many times on land.

The possession of the Great Lakes was of the
utmost importance to both the English and the
Americans.

Ever since the Revolution the English had kept
a naval force on these lakes.   They had hoped
that some time they might be able to extend the
Canadian territory along the Great Lakes and
down the Mississippi to New Orleans.   This would
give them the possession of the great west.

Many prosperous towns and trading posts were
scattered along the Canadian shores.   To capture
some of these was the task given to the American
army.

The campaign was opened by General William
Hull. With two thousand men he crossed the
Detroit River, and marched into Canada.

After a few skirmishes with the Indians, he fell
back to the fort at Detroit. Then, without firing
a single gun, he gave up this fort to the English.
This surrender was a great loss to the Americans for many reasons.

There was, in the west,
a bold Indian warrior
whose name was Tecum-
seh. He had a brother
whom the Indians called
the Prophet, because he
was a medicine man and
could do wonderful things.

These two Indians wished

TECUMSEH.

to form a union of all the
tribes from Canada to the Gulf of Mexico. They
hoped that in this way they might prevent
the white settlers from taking their hunting
grounds.

"The white men are continually driving the red

people toward the west ; by and by we shall be driven into the Great Water," they said.

The governor-general of Canada made the Indians many promises, and tried to incite them against the United States. In this way he persuaded many warlike tribes to give aid to the English. Tecumseh himself crossed into Canada and joined the British army under General Proctor.

After Hull's surrender of Detroit, the British and Indians took possession not only of that fort, but also of Fort Dearborn, where Chicago now stands. The territory of Michigan was completely in their hands, and the settlers along the lakes and all through the north- west were at the mercy of the Indians.

WILLIAM HENRY HARRISON.

General William Henry Harri- son tried to regain Detroit. His advance guard was met and de- feated at the River Raisin, a few miles south of Detroit. Every American prisoner was murdered by the Indians; and for years after- ward the River Raisin was a name of horror.

The Americans felt that something desperate must be done. The first great thing to be gained was the control of the lakes.

At this time nearly the whole of the western country was a wilderness. The only way of moving men and supplies from place to place, was by the use of boats on the lakes and water courses.

On Lake Ontario a small fleet had been built, and a skirmish or two had been fought. But the thing of most importance was the control of Lake Erie. This would not only give back Detroit to the Americans, but would also be the means of recovering the whole of the Michigan territory.

The task of building a fleet and driving the English from the lakes was given to Lieutenant Perry.

At the beginning of the war he had left his quiet home in Newport, and had hurried to Washington to ask for active service.

He was promised the first vacancy, but in the meantime he was ordered to protect the harbors of Long Island Sound with a flotilla of gunboats.

During the year 1812 he performed this duty

faithfully, all the while drilling his men, in hopes of being intrusted with a larger responsibility.

VIII.—Oliver Perry Builds a Fleet.

In February, 1813, Lieutenant Perry was ordered to go to Lake Erie. He was to take with him, from his gunboats, the men whom he thought best fitted for the service and report to Commodore Chauncey, who was in command of the squadron on Lake Ontario. The American headquarters, on that lake, were at Sacketts Harbor.

It was almost impossible to reach the place. From the Hudson River to the shores of Lake Ontario, was a vast wilderness. No road had been cut through it; none but Indians could follow the difficult trails.

The only route known to the white men was along the Mohawk River to Lake Oneida, then by the Oswego River to the little village of Oswego on Lake Ontario. To transport men and arms along this route was a great task, requiring much time, skill, and patience.

Oliver Perry was a man of action.   On the very
day that he received his orders, he started fifty
men to Lake Ontario, and the next day fifty
more.

On February 22d, in the coldest part of winter,
he left his home and his young wife in Newport,

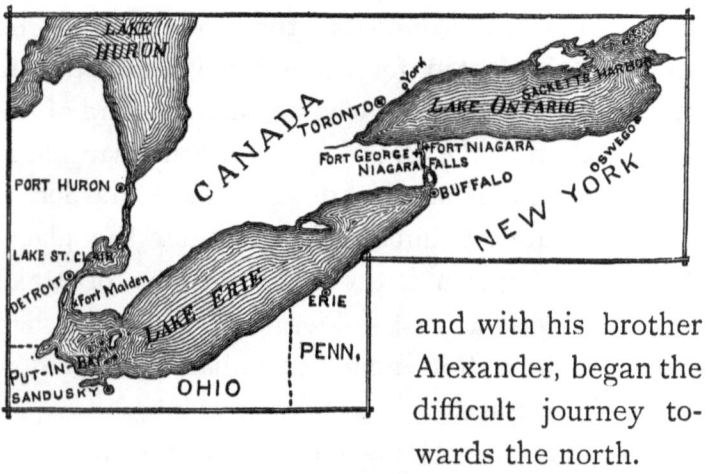

and with his brother
Alexander, began the
difficult journey to-
wards the north.

Sometimes they traveled in rude sleighs over the
roughest of roads.   Sometimes, when the river
was not too full of ice, they embarked in canoes.
At other times, they could only go on foot through
the thick underbrush.   On all sides was a vast

wilderness, inhabited only by wild beasts and unfriendly Indians.

At Oswego, they embarked in boats and followed
the shore of Lake Ontario to Sacketts Harbor.
On one side of them was the dreary inland sea
full of tossing white caps and overhung by the
leaden sky of winter.   On the other side lay the
trackless forest.

To relieve their loneliness, they occasionally fired
a musket.   The echoes would roll along the shore,
growing fainter and fainter.   This only made the
silence which followed seem greater than before.

A cold rain began to fall, and by the time they
reached Sacketts Harbor they were drenched to
the skin.

On March 16th, Lieutenant Perry set out for
Lake Erie.   Upon reaching the harbor at Erie he
found that twenty-five ship carpenters had already
begun work on three gunboats and two brigs.
Fifty more carpenters had started four weeks
before from Philadelphia, but had not yet arrived.

The task which lay before Oliver Perry seemed
almost an impossible one.   Mechanics, seamen,

guns, sailcloth,—everything needed for the ships must be brought hundreds of miles through a wild and half-settled country.

But by the end of the summer, a fleet, which seemed to have been built by magic, was ready to meet the English. Six months before, the timbers used in building the vessels had been growing trees; the iron that held these timbers together was either in the mines or in warehouses or farmers' barns, in the shape of plowshares, axes, or horseshoes.

The shipbuilders had come through the wilderness from Philadelphia. The guns, ammunition, and rigging had been brought in ox-wagons, hundreds of miles over almost impassable roads.

CAPTAIN JAMES
LAWRENCE.

While Perry was building this fleet, a sad event had taken place on the sea. The British frigate *Shannon* met and captured the American frigate *Chesapeake*, June 1, 1813, near Boston harbor.

Captain Lawrence of the *Chesapeake* fought bravely, but, in the battle, was mortally wounded. As he was being carried below, his last words were: "Don't give up the ship !"

The Secretary of the Navy sent word to Lieutenant Perry to name one of the vessels of his new fleet the *Lawrence*, after this gallant captain. Lieutenant Perry therefore gave this name to his flagship.

By the 10th of July the fleet was ready for sea, but there were only officers and men enough to man one ship. Several of these were ill with fever.

Lieutenant Perry wrote many letters to General Harrison, Commodore Chauncey, and the Secretary of the Navy.

"Give me men, and I will acquire both for you and for myself honor and glory on this lake, or die in the attempt," he said.

By the end of July he had over four hundred men for his nine vessels. But, as he said, they were a "motley crew" of regular soldiers, negroes, and raw recruits. During the battle which followed, over a hundred of these men were too sick to be of any use.

The English fleet of six vessels was commanded

by Captain Barclay.   In his crews were over five
hundred men and boys.

IX.—"We Have Met the Enemy and They are Ours."

Early in August the American squadron left the
harbor of Erie, and sailed to Put-in-Bay, an
island not far from the west end of the lake.

The British squadron was in the harbor of Fort
Malden, nearly opposite on the Canadian shore.

On the morning of September 10, 1813, from
the masthead of the *Lawrence*, the English fleet
was seen approaching.

As the Americans were sailing out to battle,
Lieutenant Perry gathered his men together and
talked to them about the courage they would need.

He showed them a large blue flag, bearing in
white letters a foot high the words: "Don't give
up the ship!"

"My brave lads," he said, "this flag bears the
last words of Captain Lawrence.   Shall I hoist it?"

With one voice, the men shouted: "Aye, aye, sir!"

As the bunting was run up on the *Lawrence*, cheer upon cheer came from every vessel of the American squadron. The men were then sent to their quarters, and every one quietly waited for the beginning of battle.

It was a beautiful morning. The sky was cloudless, and there was hardly a ripple to disturb the lake. The English vessels were newly painted, and gayly adorned with flags. Every sail shone in dazzling whiteness in the sunlight.

At half-past ten a bugle was heard from the English flagship, which was followed by cheers from the other vessels. Across the water the Americans could hear the strains of the English national air played by a band.

On the *Lawrence* all was still. With determined faces the men stood by the guns.

Lieutenant Perry knew that a great responsibility was upon him. He knew that, should he lose the battle, General Proctor and Tecumseh, with five thousand soldiers and Indians, were ready to

cross the lake, and take possession of the southern
shore. All through that part of the country,
anxious men, women, and children were waiting
to flee from their homes, if the dreaded Indians
came upon them.

These things Lieutenant Perry knew. He
passed along the deck, carefully examining every
gun. He had a word of encouragement for each
gun crew.

Seeing some of the men who had fought on the
Constitution, he said, "I need not say anything to
you. You know how to beat those fellows."

As he passed another gun, commanded by a crew
that had served in his gunboat flotilla, he said:
"Here are the Newport boys! They will do their
duty, I warrant."

In this way he filled all his men with a great
earnestness, and a determination to conquer or die.

While the two squadrons were yet a mile apart,
the English sent a cannon ball skimming over the
water. For some time there followed a vigorous
firing from both sides.

As the English guns could carry farther than

those of the Americans, Lieutenant Perry brought his flagship into close quarters. The other American vessels were some distance behind.

The whole British squadron then opened fire upon the *Lawrence*.

At the end of an hour of this unequal battle, the condition of the *Lawrence* was pitiable. One by one the guns had been disabled. Finally only one on the side toward the enemy could be used. The rigging was damaged, the spars were shattered, and the sails were torn into shreds. Eighty-three men had been killed or wounded.

Two musket balls passed through Lieutenant Perry's hat, and his clothing was torn by flying splinters.

One heavy shot crushed into the large china closet, and smashed every dish with a great clatter. A dog, that had been locked up there, startled by the noise, added to the tumult by howling dismally.

Several times the *Lawrence* barely escaped being blown up. Two cannon balls passed entirely through the powder magazine.

Even the wounded men crawled upon the deck to lend a feeble hand in firing the guns. It was Oliver Perry himself, however, that loaded and fired the last gun of the *Lawrence.*

Lieutenant Perry at last determined to change his flag from the *Lawrence* to the *Niagara.* A breeze had sprung up, which enabled this vessel to come near to the helpless *Lawrence.*

The first lieutenant was left in command of the *Lawrence*, with orders to hold out to the last. Then with his brother Alexander and four seamen, Lieutenant Perry got into a rowboat. Just as they were shoving off, a seaman on the *Lawrence* hauled down the blue flag, bearing the motto, ''Don't give up the ship!'' He rolled it up and tossed it to Perry.

The smoke of the battle was so dense that the rowboat had nearly reached the *Niagara* before it was seen by the English. Then a shot was sent which went straight through the boat's side.

Taking off his coat and rolling it up, Perry quickly thrust it into the hole which the ball had made. This kept the boat from sinking.

As he stepped upon the deck of the *Niagara*, Perry ordered the blue flag to be hoisted. Just at this moment the *Lawrence* surrendered.

The English gave a cheer, thinking they had won the battle. They were not able, however, to

THE BATTLE OF LAKE ERIE.

board and take the *Lawrence* at once, and so she drifted away. When safely out of range her colors were rehoisted.

Bringing the *Niagara* into position, Lieutenant Perry fired a terrific broadside into one of the English vessels. Then he sailed quickly to another and did the same thing.

The other American vessels followed this example, and a terrific battle followed.

In just fifteen minutes the English surrendered. Two vessels of their squadron attempted to escape, but were soon overtaken and captured.

Lieutenant Perry was determined that the formal surrender should take place on the *Lawrence*. So once more he lowered his flag, and jumping into a boat, made for his first flagship.

When he stepped on board the *Lawrence* not a cheer was heard. The handful of men that were left silently greeted their commander.

Few of them were uninjured. Some had splintered arms and legs. Others had bandages about their heads. Their faces were black with powder.

The English officers came on board to present their swords to Perry. With quiet dignity he returned each one.

He then took from his pocket an old letter. Using his cap for a desk, he wrote with a pencil his famous dispatch to General Harrison:

"We have met the enemy and they are ours. Two ships, two brigs, one schooner, and one sloop. Yours, with very great respect and esteem,

"O. H. PERRY."

X.—What Perry's Victory Accomplished.

The battle on Lake Erie was the beginning of the end of the war. The news of the victory caused great rejoicings all over the country. In all the principal towns there were meetings, bonfires, and torchlight processions.

General Harrison could now take his army into Canada. No time was lost. He hurried over four thousand men to the lake, where Perry's fleet waited to take them across.

The main body of the British army, under General Proctor and Tecumseh, was at Fort Malden. Upon landing there the Americans found that the enemy had fled, having burned the forts, barracks, and stores.

General Harrison followed the English up the left bank of the Detroit River. The fort at Detroit was surrendered without any resistance, and the English retreated along the St. Clair Lake and up the Thames River.

The Americans steadily pursued them. Perry,

with his fleet, followed the army, carrying the baggage and provisions.

He became so excited over the chase that he could not remain quietly on his ships. So, leaving them in charge of one of his officers, he went ashore and offered his services to General Harrison as aid-de-camp.

As he joined the army he was met with cheers of welcome from the soldiers. General Harrison afterward said : "The appearance of the gallant Perry cheered and animated every soldier."

Following the English some distance up the Thames, the Americans finally overtook them. They were drawn up in line of battle on a narrow strip of land which lay between the river and a large swamp.

The American cavalry made a bold dash through these lines, and the enemy was soon routed. Over sixty British and Indians were killed, and six hundred troops were made prisoners. General Proctor made his escape, but Tecumseh was killed.

The death of this great chief severed forever the

tie which bound the Indians to the English. Soon afterwards all the tribes of the northwest declared submission to the United States. The white settlers in the region about the Great Lakes were thus freed from their fear of the savages.

During the battle of the Thames, the soldiers greatly admired the fine horsemanship of Oliver Perry. He rode a powerful black horse, with a white face, that could be seen from all parts of the field.

Once, when riding swiftly to carry out some orders of the general's, the horse plunged into the deep mire to his breast. Perry pressed his hands on the pommel of the saddle, and sprang over the horse's head to dry ground.

Relieved from the weight of his rider, the horse freed himself and bounded forward. Perry clutched the mane as he passed and vaulted into the saddle, without stopping the animal's speed for a moment. As he passed the soldiers, many cheers arose.

On October 7, 1813, Perry returned to Detroit, and from there started back to his home in Newport. The people hailed him with joy, and enough could not be said in his praises. Even Captain Barclay of the English fleet called him "The gallant and generous enemy."

His journey to Newport was indeed a triumphal one. In every town that he passed through, business was stopped and the schools were closed so that all could have a glimpse of the hero of Lake Erie. Processions accompanied him from town to town.

On November 18th, he reached his home in Newport. Bells were rung, all the ships were adorned with flags, and salutes were fired in his honor.

GOLD MEDAL AWARDED BY CONGRESS.

On November 29th, he received his promotion to the rank of captain. At that time this was the highest rank in the American navy. A gold medal was also given to him by Congress.

In the following January he made a visit to Washington, where he was publicly entertained by the President and citizens.

In August, 1814, he was ordered to command a new frigate named the *Java*. He hastened to Baltimore, where this vessel was to be launched.

On the 11th of September, Lieutenant Macdonough, who was in command of the American squadron on Lake Champlain, gained a decisive victory over the British near Plattsburg. Everything at the North seemed now to be favorable to the Americans; but it was not so at the South.

While Captain Perry was waiting at Baltimore, the British had sailed up the Potomac with an army and a fleet. They captured Washington, and burned the capitol, the White House, and some of the other public buildings.

Being so successful in this, they made a like attempt upon Baltimore, but were driven back. They then blockaded Chesapeake Bay.

Just at this time, Congress passed a bill to fit out two squadrons of fast-sailing vessels. These were to cruise near the English coasts and destroy the commerce between the different ports.

Captain Perry was ordered to leave the *Java* and command one of these squadrons. But before he could sail for England, peace was declared. A treaty with that country was signed December 24, 1814.

XI.—ON THE MEDITERRANEAN AGAIN.

While the United States had been at war with England, trouble had again arisen with the Barbary States. None of these countries had been so annoying as Algiers. The ruler, or Dey, of Algiers knew that every American naval vessel was busy fighting the English. He therefore thought this a good time to burn and plunder the merchant ships. He also demanded large sums of money in return for his captured prizes and prisoners.

But no sooner was peace concluded with England, than Congress declared war with Algiers. A squadron was sent to the Mediterranean, commanded by the brave Stephen Decatur, and he

soon compelled the Dey to sign a treaty with the
United States.

In this treaty the Dey promised to give back all
the American property he had captured. If there
was anything that he could not return, he was to
pay for it at its full value. He was also to release all
the Americans he held as prisoners, and give up,
forever, all claim to tribute money from the United
States.

When the consuls of other countries heard of
what Decatur had accomplished, they tried to persuade the Algerine ruler to make the same terms
with them. Then the Dey was sorry that he had
"humbled himself" before the young republic, and
he declared that he did not consider the treaty
binding.

Congress therefore thought it wise to strengthen
the American squadron in the Mediterranean, in
order that this trouble should be settled.

Captain Perry was ordered to take the *Java* and
sail at once for Algiers. On January 22, 1816, he
set sail, and in March he joined the American
vessels off the eastern coast of Spain.

Upon arriving at Algiers, they found that the Dey had just received a large amount of tribute money from an English fleet. This made him very unwilling to talk about treaties.

The English fleet had not only brought money to pay for the release of English prisoners, but also had brought vast sums from the governments of Naples and Sardinia to buy the freedom of their enslaved countrymen.

Twelve hundred captives were freed in this way, and put aboard the English vessels. There were people of all ages, clothed in rags. Some had been taken while young and now were old men, with gray hair and beards.

The Dey refused to treat with the American commander, and the Americans would have destroyed the Algerian fleet and bombarded the town at once, but for an article in the treaty which Decatur had made. This article stated that when either side should become dissatisfied with the treaty, three months' notice should be given before actual fighting began.

While waiting for these three months to pass,

the American squadron cruised about the Mediterranean and visited the other Barbary States. The commander wished to show the rulers of these states that our country had a navy which could protect our commerce.

After this the fleet sailed along the southern coast of Europe. There was no vessel which attracted more admiration than Captain Perry's *Java*. To visit this ship was, indeed, a pleasure.

The captain was a courteous host, and always made his guests welcome. Everything on the ship was in order, and ready for instant use. The discipline of the crew was perfect.

Being a good musician himself, Captain Perry had the finest band in all the fleet. He took a personal interest in each one of his men, and was always ready with a word of praise when he saw it was deserved. He gave the midshipmen lessons in navigation, and saw that they had lessons in Spanish and French and in the use of the sword. They were even taught to dance.

Whenever it was possible the men were allowed

to go on shore, in order that they might visit the places of interest.

By January, 1817, the Dey of Algiers finally came to terms and signed a new treaty, agreeing to the conditions required by the United States. Captain Perry was soon afterwards ordered to sail for America, carrying this new treaty with him.   In March he arrived at Newport.

XII.—Captain Perry's Last Cruise.

After so many months of cruising, Captain Perry was very glad to be again in his own country.

He spent the next two years quietly at home with his family.   He built a snug little cottage in Narragansett, on the old Perry estate.   This was the same farm that had been purchased by the young Quaker, Edmund Perry, so many years before.   Here the family spent the summers.

Captain Perry was always fond of life in the country.   He took many long rides on horseback. Besides his horses, he had many other pets on the farm.   He and his three little sons spent a great deal of time taking care of them.

The winters were passed in the house at Newport.

These were the happiest years of Oliver Perry's life, and he could not help but be sorry, when, on

CAPTAIN PERRY'S RESIDENCE AT NEWPORT.

March 31, 1819, he received a summons to go to Washington.

Upon arriving there, the Secretary of the Navy told him of an expedition that the government wished him to undertake.

He was to go to Venezuela, on the northern coast of South America.   This was a new republic which had formerly been a colony of Spain. Its people were still fighting for their independence, just as the people of the United States had fought against the king of England.

Small, fast-sailing war vessels, called privateers, had been fitted out by this republic. These vessels were designed to capture Spanish merchant ships, and were allowed to keep all the money that was obtained from the prizes.

But it was not the Spanish ships alone which suffered from these privateers. The desire for prize money led them to attack ships of other nations. The American merchants had met with many losses in this way.

Captain Perry was to present claims for these losses, and also to persuade the president of Venezuela to keep his privateers from preying on American commerce. For this expedition, Perry was to have two vessels, the sloop *John Adams* and the schooner *Nonsuch*.

On July 15, 1817, he arrived at the mouth of the Orinoco River. Here he was obliged to take the small schooner in order to go up the river and reach the town of Angostura, which was then the Venezuelan capital. He sent the *John Adams* to Port Spain, on the island of Trinidad, one hundred and fifty miles away. This vessel was ordered to wait there for his return.

The voyage up the Orinoco was an interesting one. All along the shores were vast tropical forests with overhanging trees full of birds of brilliant colors. Luxuriant vines were festooned from limb to limb. Flowers of all colors grew everywhere.

On the other hand, the trip was full of hardships. The heat was fearful and the sand-flies, gnats, and mosquitoes were almost unbearable.

Soon after reaching Angostura many of the crew were taken ill with yellow fever, but Perry would not leave until his mission was accomplished. After three weeks of delay, he succeeded in getting the promises for which he had come.

The schooner then sailed down the river, reaching the mouth on August 15th. On account of a high sea, to cross the bar that night would be a dangerous undertaking, and the vessel was therefore anchored until morning.

During the night, the wind freshened so much that the spray dashed into the cabin where Captain Perry was sleeping.   In the morning he awoke with a cold chill and symptoms of yellow fever.

Every effort was made to reach the *John Adams* as soon as possible.   Captain Perry grew rapidly worse.   In the intense heat, his little schooner cabin was most uncomfortable.

The winds were unfavorable and the progress of the little vessel was slow.   When within a mile of the *John Adams*, Captain Perry died.   This was on his thirty-fourth birthday, August 23, 1819.

He was buried on the island of Trinidad with military honors, and the *John Adams* brought back the sad news to the United States.

His death was regarded as a national calamity. The government sent a war vessel to bring his body home.   He was finally laid to rest at Newport, where a granite monument marks his grave.

The feelings of his fellow officers were well expressed by Stephen Decatur.   Upon hearing of Perry's death, he said: "Sir! The American navy has lost its brightest ornament!"

THE STORY OF

ADMIRAL FARRAGUT

THE STORY OF ADMIRAL FARRAGUT.

I.—CHILDHOOD.

On July 5, 1801, in a rude cabin in Eastern Tennessee, David Glasgow Farragut was born.

It was a wild and lonely place. For miles around the little farm, nothing could be seen but woods. Few sounds could be heard save the singing of birds and sometimes the cries of wild beasts.

There was already one child in the family, a boy, whose name was William.

George Farragut, the father, was a brave man. He was a Spaniard, and had come to America during the Revolutionary War.

He was a lover of liberty, and for that reason he had taken up arms with the colonists to help them win their independence from England.

After the close of the war, he had married a hardy frontier girl, and had come to this wild place to make his home.

His life on the little clearing in the backwoods was one of toil and frequent hardships. Every day he was busy chopping down trees, planting crops, or hunting in the great forest.

The young wife, Elizabeth, was also busy, keeping her house and spinning and making the clothes for herself, her husband, and her children.

Little David Farragut grew strong very fast.

He and William had no playmates, but they liked to run about under the trees. They could not go far from the cabin, however, as there were both wild beasts and Indians in the woods.

Sometimes the father would be away for several days, hunting wild game for the family to eat. At such times, the mother and children would be left alone.

One day a band of Indians came and tried to enter the cabin. The mother sent the boys into the loft, where they crouched down close to the roof and kept very still. Then, for hours, she guarded the door with an axe, until, at last, something frightened the Indians and they went away.

When little David was about seven years old, his father was appointed by the government to command a gunboat on the Mississippi. As his headquarters were to be at New Orleans, the family moved to a plantation on the banks of Lake Pontchartrain. This lake is near the city.

When not on duty on the gunboat, George Farragut was very fond of sailing on the lake. He had a little sailboat in which he would take the children, even in severe storms.

Sometimes the weather would be so bad that they couldn't come home; and then they would sleep all night on the shore of some island. The father would wrap the children in a sail, or cover them with dry sand to keep them warm.

One day a neighbor told him that it was dangerous to take the children on such trips. George Farragut replied, "Now is the time to conquer their fears."

When fishing in the lake one morning, George

Farragut saw a boat in which there was an old man all alone. Pulling alongside, he found that the stranger had become unconscious from the heat of the sun.

He was taken to the Farragut home, and, although he was nursed for some time with the greatest of care and everything was done for him that could be done, yet he grew no better.

Finally Mrs. Farragut also was taken very ill, and in a few days both she and the stranger she had nursed so tenderly, died. This was a sad day for the family of George Farragut.

Not long after the funeral, a stranger called at the Farragut house. He said that his name was David Porter and that he was the son of the old gentleman who had died there. He thanked George Farragut for his kindness to his father, and offered to adopt one of the Farragut boys.

There were now five children in the family, and David's father was very glad to accept this offer. The oldest son, William, already had a commission as midshipman in the navy, and so it was decided that David should be the one to go.

Captain Porter was at that time the commander of the naval station at New Orleans. His handsome uniform, with its belt and shining buttons, seemed very attractive to little David, and he was eager to go with his new guardian.

David spent a few months with the Porter family in New Orleans. Then Captain Porter took him to Washington and placed him in school there.

One day David was introduced to a great man, the Secretary of the Navy. He asked the boy many questions, and was so pleased with his intelligent answers that he said to him, "My boy, when you are ten years old I shall make you a midshipman in the navy."

This was a proud moment for little David Farragut. The great man did not forget his promise. The appointment came six months before the time that was named. It was arranged that the lad should go with Captain Porter in the frigate *Essex*.

It was several months, however, before the vessel was ready to sail. In the meantime, David attended a school in Chester, Pennsylvania.

II.—The Little Midshipman.

For a long time England had been at war with France. British men-of-war and privateers were in the habit of attacking any vessel going to or from the ports of France. More than this, the British government claimed the right to search American vessels to see whether any English sailors were on board.

Nor was this the worst. Numbers of American seamen were falsely accused of being English deserters, and every year many were taken from their own vessels and forced to serve on British ships.

The Americans tried to induce the British government to cease this unjust treatment. They tried to settle the matter peaceably, but the British were haughty and overbearing and would not agree to give up any of their claims.

On June 18, 1812, things had gone so far that our country was obliged to declare war against Great Britain. A squadron was fitted out and ordered to cruise along the Atlantic coast, in order to protect American vessels from the British.

Captain Porter's vessel, the *Essex*, was to be one of this fleet. It was not ready, however, to sail with the others; but orders were given that it should follow as soon as possible and join the squadron in the Atlantic.

If Captain Porter could not find the squadron, he was to do whatever he thought best.

CAPTAIN DAVID PORTER.

On October 28, 1812, the *Essex* sailed down the Delaware River, and through the bay into the ocean. There was a pennant flying from the mast-head on which were the words, "Free Trade and Sailors' Rights" It was for these things that Captain Porter was ready to fight. By his side stood the little midshipman, David Farragut, in his shining uniform. There was no prouder boy in all America than he was on that day.

For several months, Captain Porter cruised about the Atlantic. He captured several English vessels, and then, as he could not find the American squadron, he decided to make a trip around Cape Horn, and cruise in the Pacific.

The passage around Cape Horn is one of the most dangerous in the world, but Captain Porter was not afraid. The *Essex* was one of the best ships in the navy, and the crew had been drilled very thoroughly.

Sometimes Captain Porter sounded a false alarm of fire on shipboard. This was to test the courage of the men and prepare them for accidents. Sometimes he even caused a smoke to be made. The sailors soon became so accustomed to a cry of " Fire " that it caused no confusion.

The courage of the crew was severely tried in going around Cape Horn. The weather was bitterly cold, and for twenty-one days the ship was buffeted by furious storms.

By this time the provisions were almost gone. Each man had but a small daily allowance of bread and water. Little David Farragut was having his first real experience as a sailor.

From Cape Horn, Captain Porter sailed north

along the west coast of South America, and stopped at an island near the coast of Chili. The sailors went on shore with their guns and killed some wild hogs and horses. They were in such need of fresh meat that they ate even the flesh of the horses with great relish.

For months the *Essex* cruised about in the beautiful Pacific. Captain Porter captured several English vessels, and warned American whaling-ships of danger. Some of these had been at sea for many months and had not heard of the war.

Sometimes the *Essex* would stop at an island, and the crew would go on shore to kill seals; sometimes they would anchor in shallow bays and fish for cod.

On one solitary island there was a strange post-office, a box nailed to a tree. Here passing vessels would leave messages and letters, to be taken up by other vessels that chanced to be going in the right direction.

The *Essex* stopped at this island for some time. The crew found prickly pears to eat. They killed pigeons, which the cook made into pies, and they made soup of the turtles they caught. Those were great days for David Farragut.

The *Essex* finally left this island in May, 1813. Soon more English vessels were sighted and captured. One of these was to be taken to Valparaiso, and Captain Porter put David Farragut in charge of it. The young commander was then but twelve years of age.

The gray-haired English captain was very angry at having to take orders from a boy. He tried to ignore David, and when he failed in this, attempted to frighten him. He threatened to shoot any man who obeyed David's orders, and went below for his pistols.

David knew that the American sailors were loyal to him. So he sent word to the captain that if he did not obey, he would have him thrown overboard.

After this there was no more trouble. David brought the vessel into the port of Valparaiso in safety. He soon afterward rejoined the *Essex*.

Captain Porter now decided to go to some

islands far out in the Pacific, where he could refit the ship.

As the *Essex* approached one of these islands, she was met by a canoe filled with natives. The bodies of these people were tattooed, and they were gayly ornamented with feathers. They invited the sailors on shore, and promised to give them fruit and provisions.

During the six weeks that were occupied in refitting the ship, the sailors rested on the island. David and the other boys of the crew were given lessons by the ship's chaplain each day, and when school hours were over, they were allowed to visit the islanders.

The young natives taught the American boys many things. They showed them how to walk on stilts, and how to use a spear skillfully and with ease. Best of all, they taught them how to swim. The people of this island could swim as easily as they could walk. Even the babies could float in the water like ducks.

The *Essex* left this island in December, 1813, and sailed for Valparaiso.

III.—THE LOSS OF THE ESSEX.

One day in the following February, two English war vessels appeared in the harbor of Valparaiso. The *Essex* was lying quietly at anchor, and many of her crew were on shore.

The British vessels bore down upon the *Essex* in a very hostile manner. Captain Porter was afraid they would attack him. They had no right to do this, for Chili was not at war with either England or America.

One of these British vessels was a frigate called the *Phoebe*. The other was a sloop named the *Cherub*. The *Phoebe* approached the *Essex* until she was within fifteen feet of her side.

Captain Porter, standing on the deck, hailed, saying : "If you touch a single yardarm, I shall board you instantly!" The *Phoebe* passed by with no reply.

After this, the British vessels anchored at the entrance of the harbor. They could thus keep the *Essex* a prisoner.

The vessels remained in this position for several weeks. On the 28th of March, a furious gale sprang up. The cables of the *Essex* gave way, and she began to drift out toward the English vessels. Captain Porter now made a desperate effort to escape. He set all sails and made for the open sea.

Suddenly something snapped. The main topmast came crashing down, carrying sails, rigging, and some of the crew into the water. In this disabled condition escape was impossible. The *Essex* was driven toward the shore and was finally brought to anchor within pistol shot of the beach.

The *Essex* had but four guns that would shoot as far as the cannon of the English. The *Phoebe* and the *Cherub* took a position out of range of nearly all the *Essex* guns, and then poured broadside after broadside into the unfortunate vessel.

Captain Porter and his gallant crew fought against these odds until one hundred and twenty-four of the men had been killed or wounded. Then the *Essex* surrendered.

During all this dreadful battle there was no braver officer than the little midshipman, David

Farragut. Sometimes he was carrying messages for the captain; again, he was bringing powder for the guns.

Once when going down the hatchway a wounded man fell upon him. David barely escaped being crushed to death.

Captain Porter was so pleased with his conduct that he mentioned his bravery in his official dispatches to the government.

After the surrender the wounded were removed to shore. David offered his services to the surgeons. He worked early and late, preparing bandages and waiting upon the injured men.

In speaking of this afterward, he said, "I never earned Uncle Sam's money so faithfully."

The British put all the American prisoners on board an unarmed vessel, and made them promise that they would not take up arms against the English until they had been exchanged for an equal number of English prisoners.

After this the Americans were allowed to sail for the United States. They arrived in the harbor of New York on July 7, 1814.

IV.—The Trip on the Mediterranean.

Although a prisoner of war, David Farragut was glad to get back to the United States.

While waiting to be exchanged he attended a school in Chester, Pennsylvania.

It was a strange school. The pupils had no books. The teacher, Mr. Neif, told them the things he wished them to learn, and the boys wrote them down in notebooks. They would sometimes be examined on these notes to see whether they had paid proper attention.

In the afternoons, Mr. Neif would take the boys for long walks. They made collections of minerals and plants, and learned many curious and useful facts about them.

Mr. Neif, who had been a soldier, gave the boys military drill. He also taught them to swim and climb.

David Farragut was not a handsome boy. But people liked to look at him, for his face was honest and good. He was short for his years, but he stood very erect, and held his head as high as he could.

"I cannot afford to lose any of my inches," he said.

In November, 1814, the British and the Americans made an exchange of prisoners, and David Farragut was now free to return to the navy. As a treaty of peace was made a few weeks later, he did not have to serve against the British.

During the next two years, David made but one short cruise. He was quartered, the rest of the time, on a receiving ship. This is a vessel stationed at the navy yards, where recruits are first received into the service.

In the spring of 1816, David went on a cruise that proved to be most interesting. He was ordered to the *Washington*, a beautiful new ship of seventy-four guns. This was to carry the American minister to Naples, in Italy.

While waiting at Annapolis for the minister they had a visit from the President, James Madison. Among his suite was Captain Porter, who was then a naval commissioner. He came to say good-bye to David.

The voyage across the Atlantic was one to be

remembered. The captain was very proud of his "crack" ship. He kept the crew so busy cleaning decks and scouring "bright work," that sometimes they had no food for eight hours at a time. Once all the crew were kept on deck for several nights in succession.

During the summer months, the *Washington* cruised about the Mediterranean, stopping at many places. This was a wonderful experience for David. He visited the bay of Naples. The great volcano, Vesuvius, was then in eruption, and the sight of this alone was worth the voyage.

While in the bay, the king of Naples and the emperor of Austria made a visit to the *Washington*, and a grand display was made to entertain them.

The *Washington* stopped at the coast towns of Tunis, Tripoli, and Algiers, and finally wintered in a Spanish harbor. The Spaniards were very kind to the captain. They allowed him to use their navy yard, in which to refit his vessel.

During all this cruise, the boys on the ship were taught by the chaplain, Mr. Folsom.

He was very fond of David, and in the autumn of 1817, when he was appointed consul to Tunis, he wrote to the captain of the *Washington* for permission to take David with him.

This request was granted, and David spent a delightful year with his old friend. He studied mathematics and English literature. He also learned to speak French and Italian.

He and Mr. Folsom took many trips about the Mediterranean, and these were of great benefit to him. In October, 1818, he returned to the *Washington*, in which he cruised for another year.

V.—WAR WITH THE PIRATES.

While David Farragut was at a port in the Mediterranean, he was summoned to America to take his examination for the lieutenancy. He was then eighteen years of age.

In November, 1820, he arrived in New York, where he passed his examination successfully. He did not receive any appointment, however, for some time, as there were no vacancies in the navy.

The next two years were spent with the Porter family at Norfolk, Virginia.

In 1822, he sailed for a short time on a sloop of war, that was cruising about the Gulf, of Mexico. On his return to America, he learned that Captain Porter was fitting out a fleet to cruise against the pirates of the West Indies.

These robbers had small, fast-sailing ships. They would attack unarmed merchant vessels, seize all the valuables they could carry away, and destroy the remainder. Sometimes they killed the crew; at other times they put them ashore on some desert island.

For years, Americans and English had been waging war against these pirates, but without success. With their small boats the robbers would run into the shallow bays and creeks, where no other vessels could follow them; and so they had grown bolder and bolder every year.

Ever since peace had been declared with England, Captain Porter had been a commissioner of the navy, and had made no sea voyages. But now he offered to resign his position, and drive the pirates from the sea. He said he would do this upon one condition. He must have a fleet of small vessels that could follow the pirates into their lurking places.

The government accepted his offer, and gave him orders to fit out such a fleet as he chose. He bought eight small schooners similar to those used by the pirates. To these were added five large rowboats or barges, which were called the Mosquito Fleet. David Farragut was assigned to one of the vessels named the *Greyhound*.

This fleet of Captain Porter's had many encounters with the pirates. At one time, when the *Greyhound* was off the southern coast of Cuba, some of the crew went on shore to hunt game, and were fired upon from the thicket by pirates. The Americans returned this fire without effect, and then went back to their ship.

Young Farragut was ordered to take a party of men to capture the pirates, and at three o'clock the next morning they set out in the barges.

After landing, David and his men tried to go around to a point at the rear of the place where the pirates were supposed to be. This was no easy thing to do. They had to cut their way through thickets of cactus, thorny bushes, and trailing vines. Their shoes were cut from their feet with walking over the sharp rocks; and the heat was so intense that some of the men fainted.

At last they found the pirate camp. It was deserted. The robbers had seen the *Greyhound* and the barges, and had fled to some other hiding place. In the camp, which was protected by several cannon, there were some houses a hundred feet long. There was also an immense cave filled with all kinds of goods taken from plundered vessels.

The sailors burned the houses, and carried the plunder and cannon to their boats. The prize that David himself took away was a monkey, which he had captured after a fierce struggle.

As the sailors were returning to their boats, they heard a great noise in the thicket behind them, and thought that the pirates had come back to attack them. David Farragut made a speech to his men. He urged them to stand their ground and fight bravely. Imagine their surprise and amusement at finding their foes to be thousands of land crabs, making their way through the briars!

This was only one of many encounters that the Mosquito Fleet had with the pirates. Through all the time, the American sailors suffered much from yellow fever and exposure. David Farragut afterward said: "I never owned a bed during my cruise in the West Indies, but lay down to rest wherever I found the most comfortable berth."

The pirates were finally driven from the seas. Their boats were burned or captured, and their camps destroyed.

While on this cruise, David got leave of absence to visit his sister in New Orleans. She was the only one of the family still living at the old home. It was hard for her to recognize in the stranger the boy who had left home so long before.

When young Farragut was on his way to the north and within sight of Washington, he was taken ill with yellow fever. He had nursed many a poor sailor, and had hitherto escaped the disease.

After a short time spent in a Washington hos-

pital, he was able to return home. Soon afterward, he was married in Norfolk, Virginia, to
Susan Marchant. But it was nearly two years
before he was entirely well, and strong enough
to resume his duties in the navy. In the meanwhile, he and his bride spent much time with the
family of Captain Porter.

VI.—From Lieutenant to Captain.

In August, 1825, David Farragut at last received
his commission as lieutenant. He was ordered
on board the ship *Brandywine*, the vessel which
was to have the honor of taking the Marquis de
Lafayette to France.

This great Frenchman had always been a warm
friend of the United States. Fifty years before,
he had taken a leading part in the Revolutionary
War, and had been one of General Washington's
most trusted officers.

After the Revolution, he had returned to his
home in sunny France. He had always loved
America, and in his old age he felt that he

would like to visit again the great nation which he had helped to establish. So in 1824, though old and gray, he had come back to America as the honored guest of the nation.

From one end of the land to the other, his

tour had been one grand ovation. And now that he was to return home, the good ship *Brandywine* was detailed to carry him safely across the Atlantic.

The voyage was an uneventful one for Lieutenant Farragut.

LAFAYETTE.

After landing Lafayette in France, the *Brandywine* cruised about the shores of England and in the waters of the Mediterranean for about a year.

On his return to America, Lieutenant Farragut found that his wife was in very poor health, and he obtained leave of absence from the navy, in order that he might take her to a famous doctor in New Haven, Connecticut.

During his stay in that city, he regularly attended the lectures at Yale College, for David

Farragut never wasted an opportunity for self-improvement. When his wife was better, they returned to Norfolk, where he was placed in charge of the receiving ship in the navy yard.

Most of the boys on the ship were uneducated and did not know one letter from another. Lieutenant Farragut therefore established a school on board. This proved to be of great value to these poor boys.

One boy had run away from home to avoid going to school, and he was determined that he would not study. It was only after many severe punishments that he was conquered. When once started in the right direction, he learned rapidly.

One day, seven years afterward, a fine-looking, well-dressed man stopped David Farragut on the street. On being asked his name, the stranger replied, "I have grown probably a foot since we parted, but do you not remember the boy who once gave you so much trouble?"

"Oh yes," said Farragut, "but I should never have recognized him in you."

"Nevertheless," said the stranger, "I am the

same, and am ready to acknowledge you the greatest benefactor and friend I ever had in this world of trouble."

After leaving the receiving ship, Lieutenant Farragut spent the next ten years in short cruises along the South American coast and about the Gulf of Mexico. During all this time his wife was an invalid, and her health continued to fail until her death in 1840.

For two years before her death, Lieutenant Farragut was at home on leave of absence. He could then be constantly with her and wait upon her.

In speaking of his devotion to his wife, a lady in Norfolk said: "When Lieutenant Farragut dies, every woman in the city should bring a stone, and build for him a monument reaching to the skies."

In 1841 promotion came to Farragut, and he received a commission as commander in the navy.

In 1845, the state of Texas was annexed to the United States. This brought about a dispute with Mexico concerning the southwestern boundary of the state, and the result was a short war, in which the Americans were victorious.

Commander Farragut was very anxious to serve his country in this Mexican War, and wrote many letters to the Navy Department, asking for the command of a ship. For a long time he waited in vain. When, at last, a vessel was assigned to him, it was too late for him to do his country any service. The war was about over, nda there was no more work for the navy to do.

From 1850 until 1852, he was employed in Washington, drawing up a book of regulations for the navy. As when in New Haven he had attended the lectures of Yale College, so now he attended those of the Smithsonian Institution.

SMITHSONIAN INSTITUTION.

"I have made it a rule of my life to do all things with a view to the possible future. You cannot come away from such lectures without being wiser than

when you went in," he said.   When the book of
regulations was finished, he went back to the navy
yard at Norfolk, where he gave a series of lectures
on gunnery to the officers.

About this time, England and France were at
war with Russia.   Farragut applied to Congress
for permission to visit the English and French
fleets engaged in this war.   He wished to see
whether he could learn of any improvements that
could be made in the American navy.

But Congress had other work for him to do.
There was to be a new navy yard built on the
Pacific coast, at San Francisco.   This would be a
difficult task, and one requiring the services of a
man having great knowledge and experience.   No
one was better fitted to undertake it than the
lieutenant who had been so eager to make use of
every opportunity for improvement.

In August, 1854, he was accordingly sent to
California.   Some time before this, he had married a second wife, Virginia Loyall, of Norfolk, and
she accompanied him to the Pacific coast.   There
were then no railroads across the great western

plains, and they went by ship to the isthmus of Panama. After crossing the isthmus, they embarked upon a coasting vessel, and sailed to San Francisco.

Commander Farragut spent four years in laying the foundations of what is to-day the great navy yard on Mares Island, about thirty miles from San Francisco.

Before this work was completed he was promoted to the rank of captain. This was, at that time, the highest rank in the United States navy.

In July, 1858, Captain Farragut returned home. He was given, at once, the command of the *Brooklyn*. It had been ten years since he had been on a war vessel, and he found many changes. His ship had steam power as well as sails. It was one of the first steam war vessels built for the navy.

The arrangement of the guns was the same as in the old sailing sloops. But they were much larger, and of different shape. Explosive shells were used instead of solid cannon balls.

The *Brooklyn* cruised for two years in the Atlan-

tic and the Gulf of Mexico. While on this cruise,
Captain Farragut again visited New Orleans, for
he wished to see his brother who was on duty at
the naval station there. A sorrowful welcome
awaited him, however, for his brother had died
just before his arrival. The captain sadly returned
to his ship, and soon afterward sailed home to
Norfolk.

VII.—THE QUESTION OF ALLEGIANCE.

In 1861, at the beginning of the Civil War, the
United States navy had but ninety vessels of all
kinds. Twenty-one of these were not fit for service. Only eleven of those in commission were in
American waters. The rest, which were scattered
all over the world, were recalled at once.

Some of those in far away ports were commanded by southern captains, and it would take
them several months to reach America.

It was feared that they would take their vessels
into southern ports, and turn them over to the
Confederate government. These fears, however,

were groundless, for all the vessels were safely brought into northern ports. With few exceptions, all the naval officers were loyal to the United States.

Of all these naval officers, none was more loyal than Captain Farragut. In his home in Virginia, he had watched the growing troubles with a sad heart. He was a southerner by birth, and his most tender ties were in Virginia. It was there that he had spent many years with the Porter family, and there he had numerous friends. It was there, also, that he had married and made his home.

He knew that, should war break out, he would be called upon to choose between his friends in the South, and his government in the North.

"God forbid," he said, "that I should have to raise my hand against the South." These very words showed that his decision had been made.

He felt that he owed his first allegiance to the United States government, which had given him his education, employment, and rank. He could not take up arms against the flag of his country. It was under this flag that he had received his first commission as midshipman. In that proud moment he had taken his oath to die in its defense.

On the ocean, he had seen the proudest colors lowered to the victorious stars and stripes. At Valparaiso, he had stood on the bloody deck of the *Essex*, and had seen men give their lives in order that the flag should not be hauled down. He had traveled from ocean to ocean, and had seen the star spangled banner respected by all nations.

For some weeks before the actual beginning of war, there was much excitement in Norfolk. Every day the men met together in the stores to talk over the latest news, and there were many lively discussions among them. In these meetings, Captain Farragut boldly asserted his loyalty to the government, and this caused him the loss of many of his friends.

One morning, when in discussion with some officers, one of them said to him, ''A person of your sentiments cannot live in Norfolk.''

''Well, then,'' he calmly replied, '' I can live somewhere else.''

He felt that the time for action had come. He went home at once, and told his wife that he was going to "stick to the flag," and that they must move to the North.

With sad hearts, they sailed away from Norfolk.

They went to New York, and made their home on the Hudson, in a town called Hastings.

Even there, Captain Farragut met with a cold reception. The people were suspicious of the southern officer who had come to live among them. They did not consider the great sacrifice that he had made in leaving home and friends.

Determined to do his duty, he wrote to offer his services to the government. Congress could not, at once, accept them. No minor position could be given to Captain Farragut; it must be one full of responsibility.

It was not long, however, until the government had need of his services. The Mississippi River separated two large sections of the southern states, and its control was of the greatest importance to both the North and the South.

At the beginning of the war, all the river from

Cairo, Illinois, to the Gulf, was controlled by the South. The capture of the upper forts in this section was first attempted by the North.

Large armies marched against them by land, and a fleet of river gunboats sailed down from the north to assist them. These gunboats were river steamers which the government had covered with plates of iron and armed with cannon.

While the northern river forts were thus being attacked, an expedition was planned to capture the fortifications near the river's mouth.

The strongest of these were Fort Jackson and Fort St. Philip. These were between New Orleans and the Gulf of Mexico, and their capture would give New Orleans to the North. This was considered a very important undertaking.

After much discussion, the Navy Department decided that Captain Farragut was best fitted to command this expedition. So Commander David D. Porter was sent to Hastings to talk the matter over with him. This commander was the son of the Captain Porter who had adopted David Farragut when a boy.

When Captain Farragut heard of the proposed expedition he was very enthusiastic. He hurried at once to Washington, where he was appointed commander of the Western Gulf Blockading Squadron. This was in January, 1862. His orders were to capture Forts Jackson and St. Philip, and take New Orleans.

A few weeks before this an event took place which came near making serious trouble for the United States. The Confederate government had appointed two commissioners, John Slidell and James Mason, to go to England to see if they could not get help from that country.

As it would be dangerous for them to sail in a Confederate vessel, they went to Havana, Cuba, where they took passage in an English vessel named the *Trent*.

Although they had tried to do this very secretly, Captain Wilkes, commanding a warship of the United States, heard about it, and determined to capture these men, if possible. So he pursued the *Trent* and obliged her to stop.

The Confederate commissioners refused to leave

the *Trent,* and, therefore, Captain Wilkes sent an armed force on board and carried them off. He then took them to Boston harbor, where they were imprisoned in a fort of the United States.

This act caused great indignation in England, and it was only through the prompt and wise action of President Lincoln and Congress that war was averted. An apology was made and the Confederate commissioners were allowed to proceed on their voyage without further molestation.

VIII.—The Capture of New Orleans.

On the 2d of February, 1862, Captain Farragut sailed from Hampton Roads in his flagship, the *Hartford.* This was one of the new sloops of war having both steam and sails.

All the vessels of this expedition were to meet at Ships Island, about one hundred miles from the mouth of the Mississippi. When Captain Farragut arrived there on February 20th, he found only a part of his fleet awaiting him. The other vessels arrived one by one.

This was the most powerful squadron that had ever been under an American commander. It consisted of steam sloops, gunboats, and mortar boats, forty-eight vessels in all.

An army of fifteen thousand men was at hand to assist Captain Farragut. This army had been brought from the North on transports, and was under the command of General Benjamin F. Butler.

In the channel, at the mouth of the Mississippi,

THE HARTFORD.

were heavy mud banks, made of deposits brought down by the stream. To take the large vessels over this bar was Captain Farragut's first great task. The water was so shallow that the keels of the ships would sometimes stick in the mud, and then it was with the greatest of difficulty that they could be hauled off.

It was the 18th of April before all the vessels were in the river and ready to attack the forts; and in the meanwhile, a great naval battle had been fought in other waters.

The Confederates had captured the Norfolk navy yard, and with it the United States vessel *Merrimac*, which was there at the time. They removed the masts of this vessel, and then fitted her with an iron prow, and built sloping sides over the deck, covering them with iron rails laid closely together side by side.

Five of the best Northern war vessels lay in the bay outside of the harbor.

On March 8th, 1862, the *Merrimac* attacked this fleet. She drove her iron prow straight through the side of the *Cumberland*. This vessel sank almost immediately, and but few of the men were saved.

Then the *Merrimac* attacked the *Congress*, drove her ashore, and set her on fire with red hot shot. Meanwhile, broadside after broadside had been fired at the *Merrimac;* but the shot bounded harmlessly from her sloping iron sides.

Night came on, and before attempting to destroy the other three ships, the black monster waited for the daylight.

There was consternation all through the North. How could a stop be made to this fearful work of the *Merrimac?* There was no telling what she might do on the morrow.

That same night there streamed into Chesapeake Bay a queer look-ing little vessel which had been built by a famous mechanic, Cap-tain John Ericsson. She was named the *Monitor.* She had a low, flat deck, pointed at both

CONFEDERATE FLAG.

ends. In the center was a round, revolving turret. The vessel was completely plated over with iron, and in the turret were two enormous guns, larger than any that had ever been used before.

On the morning of March 9th, when the *Mer-rimac* steamed out to finish her work of destruc-tion, a stupendous cannon ball came thundering against her black side. As the turret of the little *Monitor* swung round, there came another and another,—such a battering as never ship's side had felt before that day.

The broadsides returned by the *Merrimac* fell harmlessly on the flat deck and iron turret of the *Monitor*.

This battle lasted for nearly three hours. Neither vessel was injured to any extent. Finally the *Merrimac* withdrew, leaving the *Monitor* in possession of the bay.

In one respect, this was the most wonderful battle ever fought upon the water. It showed to all the nations of the world that new navies must be built. In one day all the war-ships in the world had become old-fashioned. The days for wooden war vessels were over.

Let us now return to Captain Farragut. As I have said, by the 18th of April he had succeeded in taking all his vessels over the bar of the Mississippi. But still greater difficulties were ahead of him.

Before he could capture New Orleans, he must pass the two forts, Jackson and St. Philip, on opposite banks of the river. First of all, however,

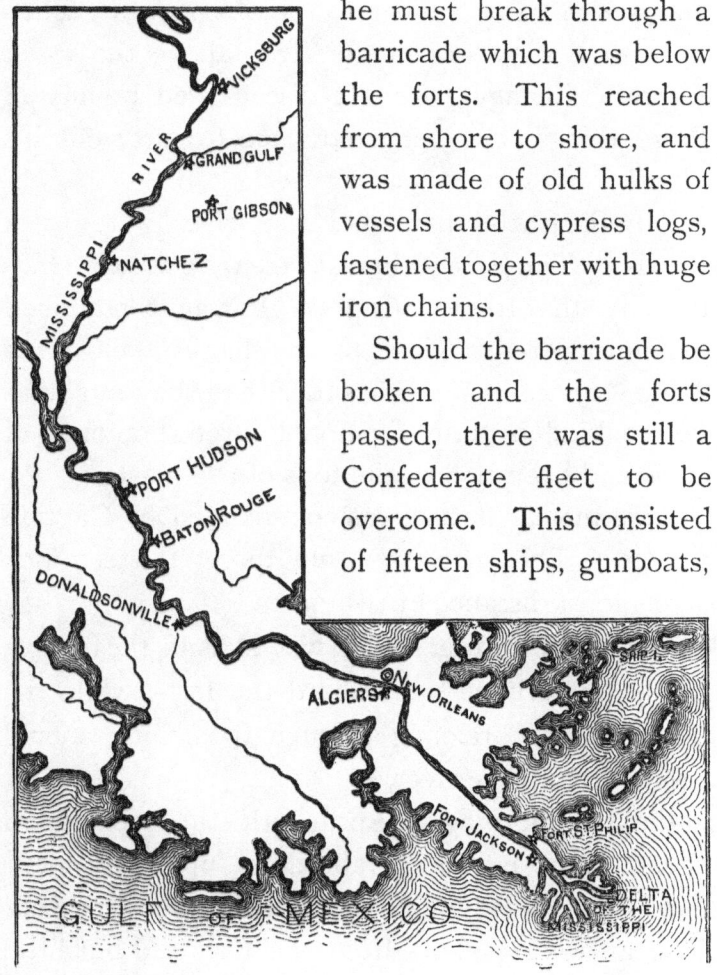

he must break through a barricade which was below the forts. This reached from shore to shore, and was made of old hulks of vessels and cypress logs, fastened together with huge iron chains.

Should the barricade be broken and the forts passed, there was still a Confederate fleet to be overcome. This consisted of fifteen ships, gunboats,

MAP OF THE LOWER MISSISSIPPI.

and steam rams similar to the *Merrimac*. They were drawn up across the river above the forts. Captain Farragut was not discouraged by any of these things, but began at once to carry out his plans.

All along the banks of the river were thick woods. The forts themselves were almost hidden by the trees. Captain Farragut stationed his mortar boats close to the banks, below the chain barricade; and, in order that they might be better hidden from the forts, large branches of trees had been tied to the tops of the masts.

This mortar flotilla was commanded by Captain Porter. The mortars could throw thirteen-inch shells for a distance of two miles.

Captain Farragut's plan was to send these mortar boats forward to bombard the forts, while the other vessels, breaking through the chains, should sail boldly up the river.

On the morning of April 18th, the shells from the mortars began to rain down upon the forts. For six days and nights this firing never ceased. The answering shots from the forts did but little

harm.   The Confederates could not take aim at
boats which they could not see.

Meanwhile, two of Captain Farragut's gunboats
crept up the river at night, and broke a passage
through the chain barricade.   Then, on the night
of April 23d, the entire fleet sailed through this
opening and boldly attacked the forts.

The whole river was at once a scene of confusion.   Every gun, both of the forts and of the
Confederate fleet, which had hastened down the
river, was sending shot and shell into the Union
fleet.

The Confederates piled every kind of inflam-
mable material upon huge rafts, set them on fire,
and sent them floating down the river.   They
hoped, in this way, to burn the invading fleet.
The river was a blaze of light.   The din from the
cannon was terrible.

But Captain Farragut and his vessels kept
steadily on.   They passed the forts, and destroyed
or captured every vessel in the Confederate fleet.
This was accomplished with the loss of but one
ship of the Union squadron.

When the news of this victory reached New Orleans, the whole city was thrown into wild confusion. Men, women, and children rushed to the levee and set fire to the goods there.

Everything that would burn was set on fire, and

sent down the river to meet the victorious fleet that was coming. Ships loaded with burning cotton, and even a half-finished ram like the *Merrimac* floated down stream, a mass of flames.

About noon on April 25th, the fleet rounded the bend of the river, and came in sight of the city. That

GENERAL. B. F. BUTLER.

same morning, the mayor of New Orleans had ordered the state flag of Louisiana to be hoisted upon the city hall.

Captain Farragut demanded that this should be hauled down. He also ordered that the stars and stripes should be raised over the buildings belonging to the United States government.

Meanwhile, Commander Porter with his mortar boats had been steadily bombarding Fort Jackson and Fort St. Philip. On April 28th, these forts surrendered, and the Union forces took possession.

On the following day, the flag of the United States was floating over the city hall of New Orleans. General Butler and his troops took possession of the city on the first of May.

On the 11th of July, on the recommendation of President Lincoln, Congress passed a resolution thanking Captain Farragut for what he had done; and a few days later he was further rewarded by being raised to the rank of rear-admiral.

IX.—THE BATTLE OF MOBILE BAY.

After the capture of New Orleans, Admiral Farragut was ordered at once to proceed up the river. He was to pass, or to attack and capture, all the Confederate forts between New Orleans and Memphis.

But for many reasons, he thought it unwise to attempt this expedition.

The increasing shallowness of the river would make it almost impossible to use his best sea-going vessels.   The upper forts were located on high bluffs, and it would be difficult to attack them from the river.

GENERAL N. P. BANKS.

Admiral Farragut knew that, should he be able to pass these forts, or even to silence their guns, he could not hold them without a large land force.   But he was too good a soldier to do anything in disobedience to orders.

In the face of all these difficulties, he passed and repassed the forts at Vicksburg and Port Hudson.   He made it plain to the Confederates that none of their batteries on the Mississippi could stop the movements of his fleet.   But he found, as he had expected, that the forts could not be held until armies came to his assistance.

A large land force under General Grant besieged

Vicksburg until it surrendered on July 4, 1863. Five days later, an army under General Nathaniel P. Banks succeeded in capturing Port Hudson.

These were the last Confederate strongholds on the Mississippi. Their capture gave to the Union forces the entire control of the river.

The command of the Mississippi squadron was given to David D. Porter, who had likewise been rewarded with the rank of rear admiral. He took charge of all the river boats of the

ADMIRAL DAVID D. PORTER.

fleet, while Farragut, with most of the sea-going vessels, sailed for the Atlantic coast.

These vessels were all in need of repairs. His flagship, the *Hartford*, which was in the best condition of all, had two hundred and forty scars from shot and shell.

After the loss of New Orleans, Mobile was the best Gulf port left to the Confederates. This city stands at the head of the broad, shallow bay of Mobile, thirty miles from the Gulf.

The entrance to the bay is very narrow, and it was protected by two strong forts,—Fort Morgan on one side, and Fort Gaines on the other.

Admiral Farragut was ordered to capture these forts. This would prevent the South from using the port of Mobile.

On January 18th, 1864, his ships having been repaired, Captain Farragut sailed again into the Gulf of Mexico.

He was anxious to make the attack early in the spring, but it was August before his fleet was ready.

In the meantime, the Confederates had made their fortifications stronger. The only channel through which the vessels could pass was near Fort Morgan. The Confederates strengthened this fort with every defense possible.

A double line of torpedoes, or submarine mines, was stretched across the channel. Above this, lay the Confederate fleet. One of these vessels, the *Tennessee*, was a huge iron ram like the *Merrimac*.

The squadron of Admiral Farragut was a strong one. There were twenty-four wooden war vessels and four ironclads like the *Monitor.*

On the night of August 4th, every preparation was made for the attack. The seamen, with determined faces, gave their messages and keepsakes to their messmates, for they hardly expected to come out of this fray alive.

Admiral Farragut, himself, made all his arrangements for the worst, though hoping for the best. He wrote to his wife, "I am going into Mobile in the morning, if God is my leader, as I hope He is, and in Him I place my trust. If He thinks it is the place for me to die, I am ready to submit to His will. God bless and preserve you, if anything should happen to me."

At sunrise the fleet moved steadily toward Fort Morgan, the stars and stripes flying from every masthead.

The four ironclads were sent ahead, close to the forts. The wooden war vessels followed, lashed together in pairs. This was done so that if one vessel became disabled it could be towed by the other.   Farragut wished to lead the fleet in his flagship, the *Hartford*, but his officers dissuaded him, and the *Brooklyn* went first, the *Hartford* following.

The admiral climbed up in the rigging, where he could command a view of the entire fleet.   As the shells from the forts began to fall about the vessels, he climbed higher and higher, in order to see above the smoke.

Fearing that a shot would cut the ropes, one of his officers climbed up to him and wound a rope around his body.   The end of this was secured to the mast.

The ironclad *Tecumseh* was now leading the fleet.   Suddenly there was a muffled explosion. The stern of the *Tecumseh* rose out of the water and she plunged bow foremost to the bottom of the channel.

At this, the *Brooklyn* stopped, and with reversed engines began to back water.   Admiral Farragut signaled, and asked, "What's the trouble?" "Torpedoes," was the reply.

This was the critical moment of the battle.

The backing of the *Brooklyn* caused confusion among the vessels following so closely upon each other. There was tremendous cheering and firing from the Confederates. They were sure that the victory was theirs.

A signal was made to the *Brooklyn* to go ahead, but she remained motionless.

What should be done? To remain there, under the guns of the fort, with the other vessels coming up behind, was out of the question. Ahead lay the dreaded line of torpedoes. Everything depended upon prompt decision.

Admiral Farragut ordered the *Hartford* to go ahead, "full speed." She passed the *Brooklyn*, and made straight for the mines that had sunk the *Tecumseh*. As they crossed the line of torpedoes, the sailors could hear them grating against the hull of the vessel. None of them exploded, however, and the *Hartford* passed the fatal line in safety.

The effect of this daring deed was wonderful. Men sprang to the guns, and the air was filled with the roar of cannon. The other vessels all followed the *Hartford* across the torpedoes, into the bay. They then attacked the Confederate fleet, and soon either captured or destroyed all but the ram *Tennessee.* This vessel had taken refuge

ADMIRAL BUCHANAN.

under the guns of Fort Morgan.

Admiral Farragut then anchored about four miies up the bay. While his men were having breakfast the iron ram steamed out boldly from the fort to attack the whole fleet.

Admiral Buchanan, the commander of the Confederate fleet, was a brave officer. Not until after a fierce combat, which lasted over an hour, was he forced to surrender the *Tennessee.*

This ended the battle of Mobile Bay. "It was one of the hardest earned victories of my life, and the most desperate battle I ever fought since the days of the *Essex*," said Farragut.

Not quite three hours had passed from the time

that Fort Morgan fired its first gun until the *Tennessee* surrendered.

With the Confederate fleet destroyed, and Mobile Bay in possession of Farragut, the forts were soon captured.

While Farragut had been winning these victories in the Gulf, a very brilliant naval battle had been fought off the coast of France.

CAPTAIN RAPHAEL SEMMES.

During the whole of the war, England had allowed the Confederates to fit out armed cruisers in her harbors, and to send them out to prey upon the United States commerce. The most famous of these cruisers was the *Alabama*, commanded by Captain Raphael Semmes. For two years this vessel had roamed the sea, burning and destroying nearly forty United States merchantmen, but always eluding the war vessels.

At last, in June, 1864, the United States war

vessel *Kearsarge* discovered this enemy in the harbor of Cherbourg, France. As it would have been against the laws of nations to fight a battle in the harbor, the *Kearsarge* remained outside to prevent the *Alabama* from getting away.

Finally on Sunday, June 19th, the *Alabama* suddenly put to sea and attacked the *Kearsarge*. The vessels were evenly matched.

The battle following was terrific. But the crew of the *Kearsarge* proved to be the better marksmen, and after an hour's furious fighting the *Alabama* suddenly gave a great lurch and plunged to the bottom of the ocean. The crew were picked up by the *Kearsarge* and some English vessels which happened to be near.

X.—WELL-EARNED LAURELS.

After the surrender of the forts, Farragut remained in Mobile Bay until the following November. His health was suffering from his labors and the effects of the southern climate.

At this time, the Navy Department requested

him to take command of an expedition against
Fort Fisher. This greatly disturbed him, and he
wrote to the Secretary of the Navy that his
strength was exhausted.

"I am willing," he said, "to do the bidding of
the government as long as I am able. I fear, however, that my health is giving way. I have now
been down to the Gulf five years out of six, and I
want rest if it is to be had."

When the Secretary of the Navy realized the
condition of his health, Admiral Farragut was
granted the much needed furlough.

Leaving his squadron in charge of an efficient
officer, he sailed north in November, 1864. As
his flagship entered New York harbor, it was met
by a committee of city officials and citizens.
Enthusiastic crowds greeted him as he landed, and
a reception in his honor was held at the custom-
house.

A few days later, a committee of citizens sent
him a request to make his home in New York.
With this request came a gift of $50,000. In
December, Congress created for him the grade

of vice-admiral.   All these honors were gratefully and modestly acknowledged by him.

In the spring of 1865 peace was declared, and Admiral Farragut went for a visit to Norfolk.   He found that many of his old acquaintances still felt very unfriendly towards him for having taken up arms against the South.   Although this pained him deeply, he said that he had never regretted having done his duty.

In 1866, the government gave him the title of Admiral.   This title made him commander of the whole American navy.   It was a rank created especially for him.   The government could give him no higher honor.

In 1867, he was appointed commander of the European squadron.   Without any request from him, the government sent permission for Mrs. Farragut to accompany him on this cruise.   On June 28th, they sailed from New York on the steam frigate *Franklin.*

This foreign cruise was more like the triumphal progress of a king than the official visit of a naval commander.   He dined with the emperor of

France and the queen of England. He visited the ports of Russia, Holland, and Belgium. He sailed again through the blue Mediterranean, visiting the places he had seen on his former cruise. A special excavation of the buried Pompeii was made for his benefit. At Malta, a grand reception was held in his honor.

But most of all, he enjoyed a visit to his father's Spanish birthplace. This was in the island of Minorca, just off the eastern coast of Spain.

He was to visit the little city on the day before Christmas. The news of his coming had spread rapidly to all parts of the island, and a general holiday had been proclaimed.

At every village on the way crowds of men and women came to meet him and bid him welcome. All along the route soldiers had been stationed to pay him honor, and give him any assistance that he might need.

Four miles from the city gates he was met by a large committee of citizens, and transferred to a handsome carriage.

The city walls, housetops, and balconies were

crowded with men, women, and children. One old man, with tears streaming down his face, shouted: '' He is ours ! He is ours ! ''

The admiral was entertained at the mansion of one of the prominent citizens. A band of music played in the vestibule, while the people came in crowds.

Early the next day, surrounded by an excited throng, he was escorted to all the places of interest. They finally went to the great cathedral, where the organ pealed forth the American national airs.

This was the last place the admiral visited before his return to America. He landed in New York, November 10th, 1868.

The following summer, he made a trip to the Pacific coast, to visit the navy yard at Mares Island. You will remember that, years before, he had laid the foundations of this navy yard.

Returning from San Francisco to the East, he was taken very ill in Chicago. By careful nursing he was able to resume the journey. But he never regained his lost strength, and his health continued steadily to fail.

The following summer the Navy Department placed a steamer at his disposal, and with his family he visited Portsmouth, New Hampshire.

This was his last sea voyage. As the ship came into harbor, he arose from his sick bed at the sound of the salute being fired in his honor.

Dressed in full uniform, he went on deck. Looking up with a sad smile at his flag flying from the masthead, he said : "It would be well if I died *now* in harness."

Shortly after his arrival he wandered on board a dismantled sloop, lying at the wharf. He looked about the ship, and, as he left her to go ashore, he said : "This is the last time I shall ever tread the deck of a man of war."

This proved to be true. On August 14th, 1870, surrounded by his family and loving friends, he died. He was sixty-nine years old.

The government sent a steam frigate to take his body to New York. On the day of his funeral, the whole city was in mourning. The buildings were draped in black. Bells were tolled and guns fired.

His body was laid in Woodlawn Cemetery.
Heading the procession was General Grant, then
the President of the United States. Following
were many military and naval officers, and thousands of soldiers.

The government erected a bronze statue in his
honor. This is in the national capital, in Farragut
Square.

Thus ends the story of the life of America's first
admiral, the story of a man who won fame and
glory by constant effort for self-improvement and
strict adherence to duty.

MONUMENT TO FARRAGUT AT WASHINGTON.

THE STORY OF

ADMIRAL DEWEY

AND THE NAVY OF 1898

George Dewey

FOREWORD.

On the 23d of April, 1898, war was declared between the United States and Spain. To understand how this came about, we must go back a great many years.

Ever since the island of Cuba was discovered by Columbus in 1492, the one thought of the Spaniards has been to gain wealth from the island without giving anything in return.

For many years, most of the Cubans have been little better off than slaves. They have always been very poor and have had to do the hard work on the plantations and in the cities. At best, they have never been able to make much more than enough to pay the taxes imposed upon them by the Spanish government.

The island has been ruled by governors sent out from Spain. Many of these have been very bad men whose only desire has been to get rich and return home. For a long time the Cubans have wished to choose their own governors, and they have frequently tried, by force, to secure the right to do this.

From 1868 to 1878, there was a rebellion known as the
"Ten Years' War." But, one by one, the insurgent bands
were scattered and their leaders killed. This war left
Cuba with a heavy debt, and the people poorer than ever.

The conduct of the Spaniards, after this war, was
more cruel and oppressive 'than before. Fifty thousand
soldiers were sent to the island to preserve peace. The
people were forced to pay for the support of this army,
and the taxes were almost unendurable.

At last, in 1895, some of the Cubans resolved to stand it
no longer. They formed an army whose watchword was
"Cuba Libre," meaning "Free Cuba," and began another
war with Spain.

The Spanish governor, General Campos, tried in vain
to conquer these insurgents, and was finally recalled to
Spain. General Weyler, who was sent in his place, proved
to be a very cruel man.

He surrounded the larger towns with trenches and
barbed wire fences, and built wooden forts or blockhouses
for his soldiers. Into these fortified towns, thousands
upon thousands of poor country people were driven, their
homes having been burned and their fields destroyed.

The sufferings of these poor people were terrible. They
were huddled together in sheds and huts without the means
even of obtaining food. Sometimes several families were
packed into one little palm-leaf hut where they had foul

air, foul water, and almost nothing to eat. Thousands of men, women, and children died from starvation and disease.

General Weyler hoped by these cruel means to starve the insurgents into submission, but the war went on just as before. Throughout the island a terrible work of destruction was carried on by both the insurgents and the Spaniards. Railroads were destroyed, and buildings and plantations were burned.

The people of the United States had heard of all these things, but for a long time did not do anything to stop them. But when the American consul at Havana, General Fitzhugh Lee, reported that many Americans were among the starving, they could endure it no longer. Food and supplies were sent through the Red Cross Society, and a little of the suffering was thus relieved.

Matters grew steadily worse in the island until President McKinley felt obliged to warn the Spanish government that they must soon end the war. He declared that if this was not done, the United States would recognize Cuba as an independent country.

Spain became alarmed at this, and, in October, 1897, the cruel Weyler was recalled, and General Blanco was sent in his place. This new governor tried to stop the war by granting to the Cubans some of the rights they demanded. He allowed them to hold some of the offices.

He released the American political prisoners, and set free
the starving country people.

But it was too late. The crops had been destroyed and
the people could not get a living. The Cuban army would

THE MAINE.

not be satisfied with anything less than independence, and
so the fighting continued.

At last an event took place which aroused the people of
the United States to a deeper interest in Cuba than before.
The United States battleship *Maine*, commanded by Captain C. D. Sigsbee, had been sent on a friendly visit to
Havana. On the 15th of February, 1898, while lying in
the harbor, she was destroyed by a fearful explosion. Two
hundred and sixty-six officers and men were killed.

President McKinley immediately appointed a committee
to find out, if possible, the cause of the disaster. These
men reported that the *Maine* was destroyed by a submarine
mine; but they could not find out who had placed it in
the harbor or who had exploded it.

There was intense excitement all over the United States during this investigation. Senator Proctor and others went to Cuba to see for themselves if the reports of the suffering there were true. When they came back, they told the people what they had seen. Senator John M. Thurston made a speech in Congress in which he said:

"I never saw so pitiful a sight as the people at Matanzas. I can never forget the hopeless anguish in their eyes. They did not ask for alms as we went among them. Men, women, and children stood silent, starving. Their only appeal came from their sad eyes.

CAPTAIN SIGSBEE OF THE MAINE.

"The government of Spain has not and will not give a dollar to save these people. They are being helped by the charity of the United States. Think of it! We are feeding these citizens of Spain; we are nursing their sick; and yet there are people who say that it is right to send food, but that we must keep hands off. I say that the time has come when muskets should go with the food."

Most of the members of Congress agreed with Senator Thurston. On the 19th of April, 1898, they passed a resolution authorizing President McKinley to use the army and navy of the United States to force Spain to abandon all claim to the island of Cuba.

Spain was not willing to give up her control of the Cubans, and therefore war was formally declared. It was only a few days until actual hostilities began.

It is the purpose of the following chapters to relate the story of the short but decisive struggle which followed. In that struggle the navy of the United States bore by far the largest share, and it is therefore of the navy and of the brave officers who commanded it that we shall have the most to say.

THE STORY OF ADMIRAL DEWEY

AND THE NAVY OF 1898.

I.—THE BATTLE OF MANILA.

On the morning of May 1, 1898, in the harbor of Manila, one of the most remarkable naval victories in the history of the world was won by the United States. The Spanish fleet, though superior in both men and guns, was entirely destroyed, and hundreds of officers and men were made prisoners. All this was accomplished by an American squadron under Commodore George Dewey, without the loss of a ship or a man. The way in which it all came about was as follows:

When war was declared between the United States and Spain, Commodore George Dewey was at Hong Kong, China, with that part of our navy which was known as the Asiatic squadron. He was at once ordered to sail to the Philippines, and capture or destroy the Spanish fleet there.

These Philippine Islands are about six hundred
miles southeast of Hong Kong.   Their capital and
largest city is Manila, on the island of Luzon.

As Commodore Dewey sailed out of the bay at

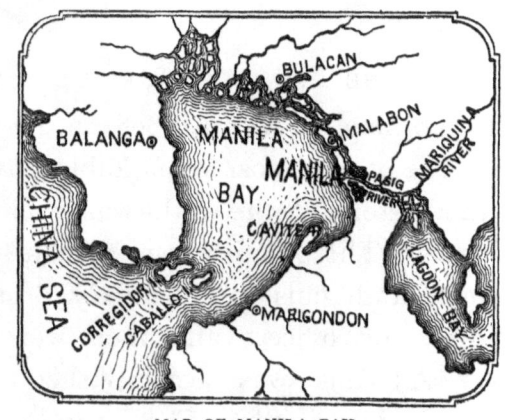

MAP OF MANILA BAY.

Hong Kong, he signaled to his fleet: "Keep
cool and obey orders."

At a little before midnight, on the 30th of April,
the American vessels in single file, led by the
flagship *Olympia*, steamed between the forts which
guarded the entrance to the bay of Manila.

In order not to be seen from these forts, all the
lights on the vessels were hidden.   Silently and

steadily the vessels moved on, unseen by the Spaniards.

All of the fleet except the *Boston* and *McCulloch* had passed in safety, when the soot in the smoke-stack of the *McCulloch* caught fire. Instantly the guns of one of the Spanish batteries were turned upon the fleet. The *Boston* and *McCulloch* returned the fire, but kept on their way and were soon out of range, having received no injury.

ADMIRAL MONTOJO.

When day broke, Commodore Dewey found the entire Spanish fleet drawn up under the protection of the batteries of the Cavité naval station about nine miles from the city of Manila. It was commanded by Admiral Patricio Montojo, one of the ablest officers in the Spanish service.

At about five o'clock, with the flagship leading, the Americans bore down upon the Spanish. Suddenly there was a muffled roar, and a submarine mine exploded. But, in the excitement, the Spaniards had fired it too soon, and no damage was done.

This was soon followed by the explosion of another mine, but again the Spaniards had been in too great haste, and the *Olympia* escaped uninjured.

Although Commodore Dewey did not know but that many other torpedoes might be in his path, he never hesitated. He had been in the battle of Mobile Bay with Farragut, when that brave commander had sailed boldly over a line of torpedoes.

Soon the guns of the batteries and Spanish fleet began to pour a storm of shot and shell at the American squadron. But, as yet, Commodore Dewey had not fired a gun.

The American sailors were wild with excitement. They had been by the guns all night, and were eager to begin the fray. Finally Commodore Dewey said quietly to the captain of the *Olympia:* "You may fire when ready, Gridley."

The flagship was now within range, and suddenly one of the great guns sent an answering shot. As its echoes went rolling across the waters, every man in the American fleet joined in the shout, ''Remember the *Maine!*'' These words were the battle cry at Manila Bay.

Slowly the American vessels steamed by the Spanish squadron in single file, pouring in deadly broadsides as they passed. Then turning, they retraced their course, drawing a little nearer to the shore. This maneuver was repeated five times. The marksmanship of the Americans was wonderful, and at the end of two hours nearly every ship in the Spanish fleet had either been sunk or was on fire.

At seven o'clock Commodore Dewey decided to withdraw out of range of the batteries, to give his men a rest and breakfast, and find what damage had been done to his own fleet. Imagine his surprise and joy at finding that not a single man had been killed, and that his vessels were scarcely injured.

At eleven o'clock the Americans returned to the attack, soon silenced the forts, and burned or captured all that remained of the Spanish fleet.

As soon as the battle was over, Commodore Dewey and his men set to work to care for the wounded Spanish sailors. They treated them like brothers, doing everything possible for their comfort.

After taking possession of the arsenal at Cavité, Commodore Dewey blockaded the port of Manila, and awaited further orders from the department of war. He knew that if the city of Manila could be captured, it would result in the loss, by the Spaniards, of the entire Philippine group.

These islands form one of the largest groups in the world, and are so rich and beautiful that they are called the "Pearls of the Ocean." They were the most important of the colonial possessions of Spain.

When the news of the victory reached the United States, there was great rejoicing all over the land, and Commodore Dewey was the hero of the hour. Congress at once gave him a vote of thanks, and promoted him to the rank of rear admiral. It also presented him with a beautiful sword, and gave a medal to each one of his men.

II.—THE BOYHOOD OF ADMIRAL DEWEY.

Who was this George Dewey who won that famous victory in the Bay of Manila? He was a native of Vermont, and had spent the greater part of his life on the sea with the American navy.

He was born in Montpelier on the day after Christmas, 1837. Montpelier was a pleasant place in which to live. There were hills to climb, and a pretty little river ran through the fields and gardens behind the Dewey home. Here George could wade, sail boats, and fish.

Although he was not fond of books, he never tired of Robinson Crusoe. With his sister Mary as Friday, he tramped many times over the hills playing that they were shipwrecked on an island.

Sometimes George's love of adventure got him into trouble. One day he read how the famous Hannibal marched, with an immense army, over the Alps in winter. The winters in Vermont are very cold, and to the ten-year-old boy the snow-covered hills around Montpelier were as good as the Alps.   So, with his sister Mary for an army, the youthful Hannibal started on his march.   The campaign proved to be too severe for faithful Mary, and she was sick in bed for a week.

When about eleven years of age, George was sent, one day, on an errand.   As it was a long distance, he was allowed to take his father's horse and buggy, and one of his boy friends for company.

On the way they came to a ford which, though usually shallow, was swollen with recent rains. When his companion wished to turn back George said, "What man has done, man can do," and drove, full speed, into the river.   The buggy, horse, and boys were soon floundering in the rapid current.

When the top and box of the buggy began to float down stream, George never lost his presence of mind.   Commanding his frightened comrade to follow him, he climbed upon the horse, and the boys reached the shore in safety.

When he returned home, George did not try to escape punishment, but administered it to himself by going to bed without any supper. But when his father came to his room and began to scold him, he thought it was a little too much. In his lisping voice he replied: "You ought to be thankful that my life wath thpared."

But George Dewey did not play all the time. His father was a good and wise man, and believed that a thorough education was one of the most important things of life. He obliged George to go to school regularly and conduct himself becomingly.

George had an experience in his first school which he never forgot. The scholars were an unruly set, and they had proved too much for several teachers. When, one day, a new master, Mr. Pangborn, arrived, the boys began as usual to make trouble. George was directed to perform some task and he flatly refused. In a moment Mr. Pangborn seized him and gave him the worst whipping that he had ever had.

Nor was this all. When he had finished, Mr. Pangborn marched the unruly George home to his father, the whole school following in the rear.

When Dr. Dewey heard the story, he told George that if Mr. Pangborn's punishment was not sufficient, he would administer more.

This settled the matter of disobedience for George. He was too manly a boy not to admire his fearless teacher. They grew to be great friends, and when Mr. Pangborn started a school of his own in Johnson, Vermont, George asked to be allowed to attend. This request was granted willingly.

III.—DEWEY AS A NAVAL CADET.

When George was fifteen years old, he was sent to a military school at Norwich, Vermont. He liked the training so well that he decided to try to get an appointment in the Naval Academy at Annapolis.

One day he told one of his school fellows, George Spalding, what he intended to do. "Why, Dewey," said Spalding, "that is what I am going to do myself." Spalding received the coveted appointment, but as he was not able to go, George went in his place.

George Spalding became a minister, and when the news of Admiral Dewey's victory at Manila reached the United States, he preached a sermon about it in his church at Syracuse, New York.

The boy who goes to the Naval School at Annapolis must be ready to work hard with both his hands and his brain. The discipline is rigid and no favors are shown or allowances made.

George Dewey was seventeen years old when he entered the Academy. He was a strong, active boy, and fond of outdoor sports. He was also a lad with whom no one could trifle.

One day one of the cadets called him insulting names. George promptly knocked him down. Soon afterward another cadet tried to test the courage of the "new boy," but received a worse thrashing than the first one had.

The cadets, however, were a manly set, and they admired George for his courage in defending his rights. Long before the four years' training had expired, George was one of the most popular members of his class. It is greatly to his credit, that, although study was not naturally easy for him, yet he graduated as the fifth in his class. This, at Annapolis, means good honest work.

George was graduated in 1858, and in order to finish his training, went on a two years' cruise to the Mediterranean in the *Wabash*. On his return, he visited his old home in Montpelier, and while there the war between the Union and the Southern Confederacy began. He hurried to Washington, where he received his commission as lieutenant.

IV.—From Lieutenant to Commodore.

Lieutenant Dewey was ordered to the steam sloop *Mississippi*, one of the Gulf Squadron, of which Admiral Farragut was the commander. Though but twenty-three years of age, the young lieutenant won the admiration of both officers and men.

When the fleet passed the forts below New Orleans, the *Mississippi* was the third in the line. All through that terrible fight, Lieutenant Dewey stood on the bridge, amid the storm of shot and shell. Whenever the guns flashed out in the darkness, the sailors could see him holding firmly to the rail, giving orders as calmly as though a battle were an everyday affair.

When the Confederate iron-clad, *Pensacola*, tried to ram the *Mississippi*, Lieutenant Dewey never lost his presence of mind. By a quick move, the *Mississippi* avoided the *Pensacola*, and passing by, poured such a broadside into the ram that her crew ran her ashore in a sinking condition. Admiral Farragut praised the young lieutenant warmly for his brave conduct in this battle.

About a year later the *Mississippi*, while trying to pass the forts at Port Hudson, ran aground. The vessel was directly in range of the enemy's batteries, and there was no hope of saving her. Shot after shot came crashing through her sides.

The officers who had the task of saving the crew did not return to the *Mississippi* after their trip to a place of safety. The rest of the crew were saved by Lieutenant Dewey. He was obliged to make several trips to the nearest vessel before he had placed all of the crew out of danger.

When no one was left on board but Captain Smith and himself, they set fire to the *Mississippi* in five places, so that she should not fall into the hands of the enemy.

As Dewey and the captain were about to get into their boat, Captain Smith said: "Are you sure she will burn, Dewey?"

"I will take one look more to be sure," replied the brave lieutenant; and, at the risk of his life, he made his way back and saw that the fires they had started were making good headway.   He then rejoined the captain, and they pulled away from the burning ship.

After the loss of the *Mississippi*, Lieutenant Dewey was ordered to one of Admiral Farragut's dispatch boats.   The admiral often came on board and was very friendly to the young lieutenant.

In 1864, Dewey was assigned to the *Colorado* as first lieutenant.   This vessel was part of the fleet besieging Fort Fisher.

During the second attack on the fort, the *Colorado* was ordered to go up close to a certain battery and silence it.   Some of the officers objected, as the *Colorado* was a wooden vessel and had already been badly damaged.   Lieutenant Dewey said, ''We shall be safer in there, and the battery can be taken in fifteen minutes.'' The attack was a success and proved that Dewey was wise as well as brave.

After the battle, Admiral Porter came to thank the commander of the *Colorado* for the work that his vessel had done. The commodore replied, ''You must thank Lieutenant Dewey. It was his move.''

Three months later he was promoted to the rank of lieutenant commander on account of the courage and ability he had shown.

After the close of the war, Dewey's father went to see Farragut in New York. The famous admiral shook Dr. Dewey's hand warmly and said, ''Sir! Your son George is a worthy and brave officer and some day will make his mark.''

In 1884 he was made captain. He did not receive the rank of commodore until 1896.

During all these years, he worked hard and did his duty faithfully. When not on the sea, he was at work on shore, teaching in the Naval Academy, making marine maps, or looking after supplies for the vessels.

Admiral Dewey's sailors are very fond of him, for although he is strict he is always just. The two things which he especially dislikes are disobedience and untruth.

On one occasion, when captain of the *Dolphin*, his lieutenant reported that one of the men had refused to perform some task on the plea that it was not his work. Captain Dewey came on deck, and, looking sternly at the man, said:

"What! you refuse to do as you are told! Don't you know that this is mutiny?" Calling for the guard, he ordered them to load their guns. "Now, my man," he said, "you have just five minutes in which to obey that order." The captain began counting the minutes, and by the time he had reached four, the order was obeyed.

At another time, while at Gibraltar, one of his sailors who had been ashore, came aboard late at night, very drunk. Next morning, he tried to excuse himself to the captain by saying that he had only had two glasses of grog, but had afterwards been sun-struck.

"You are lying, my man," said Dewey. "You

were very drunk. I expect my men to tell me the truth. Had you told me that you were drunk, I would have made the punishment as light as possible. Now you get ten days in irons for lying."

In January, 1898, Commodore Dewey was ordered to take command of the Asiatic Squadron at Hong Kong, China.

V.—The American Navy in Cuban Waters.

While Admiral Dewey had been winning fame at Manila, the Navy Department had organized two other fleets which were to be used nearer home.

One of these was called the Flying Squadron because it was composed of fast cruisers. It was stationed at Hampton Roads. From this point, it could move quickly either north or south to protect the cities on the Atlantic coast in case they should be attacked by a Spanish fleet.

The commander of the Flying Squadron was Commodore Winfield Scott Schley, later a rear

admiral. He was an experienced officer. He
had graduated from Annapolis in time to serve
all through the Civil War.

In 1884, he commanded the relief expedition
which rescued Lieutenant Greely and his explor-

ing party at Cape Sabine.
To do this, he had to
sail through fourteen hundred miles of ice-covered
ocean.

In 1891, he commanded
the *Baltimore*, stationed at
Valparaiso. One day, a
party of his sailors who
had gone on shore for pleas-

ADMIRAL SCHLEY.

ure, were attacked by a mob. Two of them were
killed and the rest were made prisoners.

Captain Schley boldly went on shore and
demanded the release of his men, and a sum of
money for those who had been killed. As he
intimated that a refusal would be followed by a
bombardment from the guns of his vessel, the
demand was granted.

Such was the man that the government had selected to command the Flying Squadron.

The other fleet was much larger, and was called the North Atlantic Squadron. It was composed of great battleships, monitors, cruisers, and torpedo-boats. This squadron was to blockade the ports of Cuba in order to prevent any foreign vessel from bringing aid to the Spanish soldiers.

This fleet was under the command of Captain William T. Sampson, who was also made a rear admiral a

ADMIRAL SAMPSON.

little later in the war. The government could well trust this important duty to Admiral Sampson. Graduating from West Point in 1861, he had served through the Civil War, and afterward, step by step, had won promotion.

During these years he had seen service in both the Pacific and Atlantic Oceans, and had occupied many responsible positions in the Navy Depart-

ment on shore.   He had also been one of the
committee that had investigated the loss of the
battleship *Maine*.

All this had prepared him for the great task of
commanding the North Atlantic Squadron.   The
prudence and judgment with which he performed
this duty proved that the government had made
a wise selection.

The people of America were still rejoicing over
the victory at Manila, when the news came that
the Spanish admiral, Cervera, with four of the
finest cruisers in the world, and three of the latest
kind of torpedo boat destroyers, had sailed from
the Canary Islands for the United States.   This
caused some alarm, and wild reports were spread
as to what these vessels might do.   Admiral
Sampson, with his fleet, was guarding the West
Indian waters, and Commodore Schley, with his
Flying Squadron, was waiting at Hampton
Roads in case Admiral Cervera should sail
north.   If the Spanish admiral could evade these
fleets, he might bombard the cities on the Atlantic
coast.

VI.—THE CRUISE OF THE OREGON.

In the meanwhile, the greatest anxiety was felt
for the United States battleship *Oregon*. When
the *Maine* was destroyed, this vessel was at the
Mare Island Navy Yard near San Francisco.
Before war was declared she had been ordered to

THE OREGON.

join the squadron of Admiral Sampson as soon as
possible.

To do this she must travel through fourteen
thousand miles of stormy sea, through the dangerous passage around Cape Horn and then up the
eastern shore of South America.

On the 14th of March, commanded by Captain
Clark, she sailed from San Francisco, entering
the straits of Magellan on the 17th of April. On

the same day that Admiral Dewey reached the Philippines, the *Oregon* arrived at Rio de Janeiro, Brazil.

Every American was full of anxiety for the great battleship. Surely Admiral Cervera would arrive in the West Indian waters before the *Oregon* could pass through them. But swiftly and steadily the great ship came on.

Finally, on the 24th of May, the *Oregon* sighted the harbor lights of Key West, and soon reached a safe port. The very next day, Captain Clark reported her ready for duty. She had steamed the length of two oceans and not a valve was broken nor a repair needed.

Much praise is due to Captain Clark for bringing his vessel such a distance in desperate haste in order to help fight the nation's battles. But we must not forget that it was the chief engineer, Robert W. Milligen, and his seventy men, who made this possible. In spite of the terrible heat in the engine rooms, these brave fellows worked untiringly to keep the great ship moving steadily day and night around the continent.

Meanwhile, on the 11th of May, an unfortunate affair had occurred in the harbor of Cardenas, on the northern coast of Cuba. Three of the American vessels blockading this harbor had been ordered to explore the bay. Suddenly the Spanish batteries on the shore opened fire. The torpedo boat *Winslow*, being nearest the shore, received most of the enemy's shells. Although bravely returning

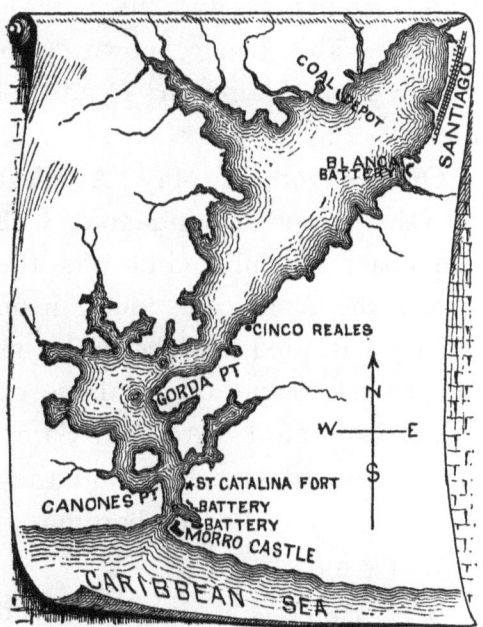

MAP OF HARBOR OF SANTIAGO DE CUBA.

the fire, the little boat was soon disabled. Five men were wounded, and Ensign Worth Bagley and four other men were killed. These were

the first Americans to lose their lives in this
war.

On the following day, the Americans heard that
the Spanish fleet had arrived at Martinique, a
small French Island near the coast of Venezuela. This being known, Commodore Schley
sailed from Hampton Roads for the West Indies.

On the 19th of May, Admiral Cervera sailed
into the harbor of Santiago de Cuba, on the southern coast of Cuba, and was there several days
before the Americans found it out. Commodore
Schley hastened at once to the mouth of the harbor so as to cut off all hope of escape for the
Spanish admiral. Admiral Sampson soon arrived
with the main squadron, and the entire fleet kept
watch, frequently bombarding the forts at the
harbor's mouth.

The Americans did not attempt to pass into
the harbor, as the entrance was strongly protected by torpedoes ; so they waited for a land
force to arrive, and attack the enemy from the
rear.

VII.—Lieutenant Hobson and the Merrimac.

Soon after Admiral Sampson arrived off Santiago, there came to him a young lieutenant, Richmond Pearson Hobson. He had a plan which he wished to propose. He said:

"There is the collier *Merrimac*. Let a volunteer crew just large enough to navigate her be selected. Then, after stripping the old ship of everything valuable, let this crew run her, after dark, into the narrowest part of the channel leading to the harbor; and there let them sink her

LIEUTENANT HOBSON.

by exploding torpedoes under her. In this way we can block the harbor so that Admiral Cerveia cannot in any way bring out his fleet."

He explained that the crew of the *Merrimac* would jump overboard as she sank, and, if possible, be picked up by a torpedo-boat or a steam launch, which should be stationed near-by for that purpose.   Lieutenant Hobson himself, bravely offered to lead this expedition.

Admiral Sampson determined to carry out this plan, and called for a single volunteer from each ship.   In spite of the danger of the undertaking, almost the entire crew of each vessel, not only offered to go, but begged to be accepted.   Finally, eight men were chosen, with Lieutenant Hobson as their leader.   At half-past two o'clock in the morning of June 3d, the *Merrimac* was headed straight for the channel.   Lieutenant Hobson stood on the bridge dressed in full uniform.   The other men were at their posts dressed in tights, ready to swim a long distance, if necessary.

The crew of the steam launch, which was following closely behind, saw the *Merrimac* swing across the channel and then heard the explosions. At the same time, the air was filled with the flash and roar of the guns of the Spanish forts and ships.

In the face of all this fire, and without even a cry of distress to guide them, the crew of the launch began their search for the heroes of the *Merrimac,* never giving it up until daylight. Then, seeing nothing but the tops of the masts of the collier, they returned to the admiral's flagship.

Of what had happened to his men in the meantime, Lieutenant Hobson himself told afterward:

"When the boat began to sink, and the Spanish shot to fall about us, I told the men to lie flat on the deck. It was due to their splendid discipline, that we were not killed. The minutes seemed hours, but I said that we must lie there until daylight. Now and then one of the men would say, 'Hadn't we better drop off now, sir?' But I said, 'Wait until daylight.' I hoped that by that time we might be recognized and saved.

"The old *Merrimac* kept sinking. It was splendid the way the men behaved. The fire from the batteries and ships was dreadful. As the water came up on the decks, we caught hold of the edges of the raft which was tied to the boom, and hung on, our heads only being above water.

"A Spanish launch then came toward the *Merrimac.* As she drew near, the men saw us, and a

half-dozen marines pointed their rifles at our heads.
'Is there any officer in that boat to receive a surrender of prisoners of war?' I shouted.   An old
man leaned out of the launch and waved his
hand.   It was Admiral Cervera.   The marines

THE MORRO CASTLE, COMMANDING THE ENTRANCE OF THE HARBOR OF
SANTIAGO DE CUBA.

lowered their rifles and we were helped into the
launch."

A few hours later, a boat bearing a flag of truce
came out to the American fleet.   It was from Admiral Cervera, and brought the message that
Lieutenant Hobson and his men were held as

prisoners, and that they were well, only two of them being slightly wounded.

Much honor is due to Lieutenant Hobson for this brave deed. But we must not forget that the lives of the crew were saved through the kindness and nobility of Admiral Cervera. Not every commander would so honor his brave prisoners, and his action has been much appreciated in America.

The sinking of the *Merrimac* did not obstruct the channel completely. The steering gear was broken by some of the Spanish shot, and Lieutenant Hobson was not able to place the vessel exactly where he had intended. However, it would be a dangerous undertaking for the Spanish admiral to pass out of the harbor at night.

Admiral Sampson sent word to the War Department, that, if an army were sent to assist him on land, they could take the city of Santiago, together with the fleet of Admiral Cervera in the harbor. Accordingly General Shafter, with a large army, landed near Santiago and began to drive the Spaniards back into the city.

Desperate battles were fought at Siboney, El

Caney, and San Juan, but the Americans steadily drove the enemy inside the fortifications of Santiago. During these attacks, the fleets helped the army by throwing shells into the city.

VIII.—The Destruction of Cervera's Fleet.

On Sunday morning, July 3d, the American ships were lying quietly outside the harbor of Santiago.

ADMIRAL CERVERA.

They were stretched in a line from Commodore Schley's flagship, the *Brooklyn*, seven miles eastward, where Admiral Sampson had gone with his flagship *New York*, in order to confer with General Shafter.

From the forts on the shore, the great ships looked like mere specks upon the horizon ; and it was hard to realize that they were grim sentinels watching every movement of the Spaniards.

The "bright work" had all been cleaned and

the men were at Sunday services, when suddenly a thin film of smoke was observed to rise behind the hills. The scene on the battleships was changed at once into one of greatest activity.

"The enemy is coming out!" was signaled in red, white, and blue from vessel to vessel, and on each deck rang out the command, "All hands clear ship for action!"

There was no confusion or noise, and every man was at his post. Powder magazines were opened, and shot and shell were being hoisted to the decks. The engineers stood waiting for the first command with every rod and wheel of the great machinery ready to move.

Meanwhile the film of smoke had become a thick cloud, and the Americans knew that soon the Spanish vessels would appear. Suddenly the flagship of the Spanish admiral was seen speeding out of the narrow channel. She passed the wreck of the *Merrimac*, and with the spray dashing high over her bows, started westward along the coast.

Close behind her came another vessel, and then another, until the six Spanish ships were all rushing wildly for the open sea. At full speed, the *Brooklyn*, *Texas*, *Iowa*, and *Oregon* bore down upon the Spanish ships. The *Oregon* gained headway so rapidly that she passed the *Texas* and the *Iowa*, and came in behind the *Brooklyn*.

Away to the right between the battleships and the shore, sped the little yacht *Gloucester*. Her captain, Lieutenant Richard Wainwright, had been an officer on the *Maine* when that vessel was blown up in Havana harbor, and so was, perhaps, most anxious of all for a chance at the Spanish.

He sent the *Gloucester* straight towards the Spanish torpedo boats, *Pluton* and *Furor*. He did not seem to mind the fact that his little yacht was no match for them, and that his decks were covered with Spanish shell. Although aided to some extent by the large vessels, the destruction of the two torpedo boats was due to Lieutenant Wainwright. He never paused in his deadly fire until both of them had surrendered. It was not long, however, until the Spanish shots began to fall about the other American ships, throwing up great columns of water.

The *Brooklyn* was the first to reach the Spanish ships and open fire. The *Oregon* hastened to assist Commodore Schley. When the Americans saw that not only the *Oregon*, but the *Texas* and *Iowa* were gaining on the Spanish, they were wild with excitement. The stokers in the engine rooms poured in the coal, and the steam rose higher and higher.

At half-past ten the battle was at its height. Great clouds of smoke settled over the water, and the roar of the guns, echoed back from the Santiago hills. Now and then anxious inquiry passed from one American crew to another; but the answer, "All right!" always came back through the din of battle.

One by one the Spanish guns became silent, and by eleven o'clock all save one of the enemy's ships had been driven ashore, and destroyed. The *Cristobal Colon* made a desperate dash for freedom, and was not overtaken until she had gone fifty miles west of Santiago. Then she surrendered, having been forced ashore.

After the battle was over the Americans bravely

went to the rescue of the Spanish sailors. They climbed the ladders and went into the burning ships, where magazines were likely to explode at any moment. They lifted the wounded men from the hot decks and took them out of the stifling smoke to their own vessels. Their boats picked up the Spaniards who were struggling in the water or trying to climb up on the shore.

The Spanish loss on that Sunday was about three hundred killed and one hundred and fifty wounded, while nearly a thousand men were taken prisoners by the Americans. The Spanish vessels were all complete wrecks. There was but one American killed and one wounded.

Admiral Cervera was a brave man. He took his fleet out of the Santiago harbor against his own judgment, because he had been ordered to do so by the Spanish government at Madrid.

Everything was against him. Many of his officers had been given their commissions because their families were rich and powerful in Spain. The sailors had not entered the navy from choice, but had been forced to do so by the government.

Many of them had been kidnapped from their homes, or from the wharves of seaport towns, and forced on board. They were ill treated and poorly paid. On the morning of the battle at Santiago they were threatened with pistols before they would go out to meet the Americans.

On the other hand, every man in the American fleet had been thoroughly trained for the work that he had to do, and was fighting for a country which he loved better than life itself. He felt that it was an honor to serve in the navy, and knew that many of his countrymen would be glad to be in his place.

Now let us see what has become of Lieutenant Hobson and his men. During all this time they had been held as prisoners in Santiago. Three days after the destruction of the Spanish fleet, arrangements were made to exchange them for some Spanish prisoners. This exchange was made between the Spanish and American lines near Santiago.

When the formalities were over and Hobson and his men approached the first American line, all the men cheered wildly and crowded one upon another for a chance to shake hands with the heroes. Lieutenant Hobson was the hero of the hour. He alone was calm, and he modestly said that any other man would have done the same thing in his place.

IX.—THE END OF THE WAR.

After the loss of Admiral Cervera's fleet, every one knew that it would be only a question of time until the city of Santiago must surrender. The American army under General Miles and General Shafter surrounded the city on the land, while the navy guarded the harbor. The Spaniards could not escape, nor could any help reach them.

The next two weeks were spent in trying to fix upon terms of surrender that would be acceptable to both sides. The only fighting was a short bombardment of the city by the warships on the 10th of July.

At last on July 17th the city surrendered. The Spaniards agreed to give up not only Santiago but also all the cities and forts east of that place, with all the soldiers and military supplies. The Americans agreed to send all these soldiers, numbering about 22,000 men, back to Spain, and pay for their transportation.

After this surrender, General Miles with an army on transport ships sailed for the island of Porto Rico, which is about four hundred miles from Cuba. As usual, the navy went along to protect the unarmed vessels and to help the army make a landing.

The first fighting was on the southern coast, near the city of Ponce, in the harbor of Guanica. Lieutenant Wainwright, with his little ship the *Gloucester*, sailed boldly into the harbor and drove the Spaniards from the shore. The Americans were then landed without the loss of a single man.

The army was divided into three divisions, and all set out for the city of San Juan upon the northern coast. They drove the Spaniards before them, taking possession of the towns and cities as they advanced.

General Miles and his soldiers were everywhere welcomed gladly, for the people of this island did not like the Spanish soldiers any better than did the Cubans.

By the 26th of July, the people of Spain had begun to realize that it was useless to carry on the war any longer. Accordingly, word was sent to President McKinley, by the French ambassador at Washington, M. Jules Cambon, that the Spanish government was ready to consider terms of peace.

President McKinley and his cabinet at once drew up a paper called a protocol, which stated what the Spanish must do before the war could be ended.

Spain was to give up all claim to Cuba, recall her officials and soldiers, and permit the people of the island to choose their own government. Porto Rico and all the Spanish islands in the West Indies were to be given to the United States. Spain was also to allow the Americans to hold the city of Manila until it should be decided, by a regular treaty, what should be done with the Philippine Islands. Five men from each country should be appointed to draw up the treaty, and in the meantime, as soon as Spain and the United States should sign the protocol, all fighting should cease.

Spain was glad to get peace, even on these terms, and the protocol was duly signed by both governments on the 12th of August. Word was at once sent to the armies and navies to cease fighting.

It was very easy to reach the American forces in Cuba and Porto Rico, but before the message could reach Admiral Dewey at Manila, it must be telegraphed to Hong Kong, China, and then sent by a dispatch boat to Manila. During the summer vessel after vessel had sailed from San Francisco, carrying the army of General Merritt to assist Admiral Dewey. War vessels and ammunition had also been sent.

On the 13th of August, not having heard that peace had been declared, General Merritt ordered a combined attack of the army and navy to be made upon Manila. The vessels opened fire upon the Spanish fortifications which protected the town, while the troops of General Merritt drove the Spaniards back into the city.   After two hours of sharp fighting the city surrendered.

The Americans did not lose a single sailor, and only twelve soldiers were killed and forty wounded. The Spanish loss was much greater.   In the afternoon the stars and stripes were hoisted over the government building and the Spanish soldiers marched out of the city and laid down their arms.

Thus with a brilliant victory, Admiral Dewey closed the war as he had opened it.

After the signing of the protocol Admiral Sampson and Commodore Schley sailed to New York with most of their squadrons to repair what little damage had been done.   When they arrived on the 20th of August the city gave them a royal welcome.   It was arranged that the warships should steam through the harbor and up the Hudson River as far as General Grant's tomb.   Thus every one could see and greet the naval heroes. The people turned out by the tens of thousands and lined the shores cheering and waving flags. The harbor and river were filled with pleasure boats adorned with flags and streamers, while cannon on the shore thundered salutes.

In all history there is not an instance of such great victories with so small a loss of men and ships as in this war with Spain. In less than three months the United States had driven the Spanish power from the western hemisphere. It had added new possessions in both hemispheres and had shown that it was entitled to rank with the most powerful nations of the earth.

As soon as the people of the United States felt that peace was assured they held great jubilees in Chicago and Philadelphia. Triumphal arches were erected under which marched the heroes of the war, cheered to the echo by their fellow citizens.

Several new battleships more powerful than any that had taken part in the recent splendid victories were launched, with imposing ceremonies, at Newport News, Virginia.

From all this it would seem that the people of the United States at last realized that at all times, whether in peace or war, the country should have a powerful navy.   This navy should be in keeping with the position that the United States has won among the nations of the world, and worthy of the brave officers and sailors who spend their lives in its service.

X.—Life on an American Man-of-War.

When a battleship is hurling shot and shell at an enemy, the brave deeds of the officers and men on board are told from one end of the land to the other; but how many people know how these men live from day to day, when the great ship is lying in the harbor, or cruising peacefully about the seas?

Who makes the lieutenant's bed and buys his food? Most people think that the government provides all that he needs; but this is not so.   He must carry his own bed linen to sea with him and arrange for his own food.

The officers choose one of their number to buy the provisions, and he must give good meals at one dollar a day for each man.   At the end of the month, every officer pays this amount out of his salary.

The first meal of the day is always eggs, and is served at any time from 7:30 until 8:30 in the morning. If ever a naval officer invites you to breakfast, he does not expect you to come to this meal. He calls a twelve o'clock luncheon break-fast, and will give you a substantial meal at that time. Dinner is served at 6 or 6:30, and, on the flagship, is accompanied by the band.

The ward-room boys who wait upon the officers are almost all Japanese. Because their names are so hard to pronounce, every one is called "Wil-liam." When the big ship is hurling shot and shell in time of battle, where is William? In the pantry washing dishes? No, indeed.

Somebody must be down in the magazine put-ting the powder on the hoists which carry it up to the guns. This is William's work. In time of fire, it is he who holds the nozzle of the hose, or who brings hammocks to smother the flames.

Now "Jacky," as the sailor man is called, does not provide his food or his bed-linen. His bed is a hammock, and it is a very different one from those we swing on our porches in summer. It is made of canvas, with ropes in the ends. He has a mattress and a blanket in his bed, and he always keeps them there.

At five o'clock in the morning the bugle calls, and Jacky has six minutes in which to scramble out of his bed and get into his clothes. Then he must roll up his hammock and stow it away. Jacky then has some hard tack and coffee before he goes to work.

From half-past five until six he does his laundry work. He wears white suits and must wash them himself ; untidiness is never excused. The clothes are then hung so as to be dry for the inspection drill which will come at half-past nine.

Then for one hour, the ship is scrubbed. Water pours over the decks in streams. Every nook and cranny is numbered, and each man has his own number to keep clean.

By half-past seven there is nothing cleaner on land or sea. The ship shines from prow to stern, and the decks are clean enough to eat from.

Every piece of metal is polished until it glitters in the sunlight.

When this is finished, Jacky has his breakfast. The government allows thirty cents a day for the rations of each sailor. The paymaster serves out food enough to last several days or sometimes a week, and if the cook does not make this last the crew must go hungry.

The sailors are divided into "messes," each mess having its own cook who is under the direction of the general ship's cook. Jacky has no table-cloth or napkins. He washes his own tin plate, cup, knife, fork, and spoon, when he has finished his hasty meal.

At eight o'clock, he is dressed for the day, and the colors go up. From then until six o'clock in the evening he is busy with different drills and duties about the ship. In the evening, from six until eight o'clock, Jacky has an easy time. It is then that he takes his ease, smoking his pipe and singing his songs.

At nine o'clock "taps" are sounded, and once more he rolls up in his hammock for the night.

Saturday is mending day, and every man must do his own work. Some of the men make their own clothes, although there is a tailor on board. In the ship's crew there are also barbers, shoe-makers, and printers.

On Sunday morning, the captain goes about the ship and gravely inspects the men, and it is then that each one tries to look his best. Then they must all attend religious services, after which they rest most of the day.

The marines on a ship-of-war are men about whom most people know nothing. A marine is not a sailor. He is a soldier who does duty on a warship. He is a kind of policeman, and sees that Jacky behaves himself. He wears a soldier's uniform and has soldier's drills.

The marines have their own mess and their own sleeping space, forming a community of their own.

Perhaps some boys and girls may think that the captain and his officers have a much easier time than Jacky or the marines. This is not so. In the first place, they had many studies to

master before they could be officers. They had
to earn a great deal about mathematics, mechan-
ical and electrical engineering, navigation, gunnery, and international law. And then these
studies are never ended; the progress that is made
in them, each year all over the world, must be
known by each officer.

The officers are responsible for the lives of the
crew and the safety of the ship. They must be
ready to think and act quickly in emergen-
cies. In hours of peril they never leave their
posts.

XI.—Some Facts about the Navy of 1898.

The Constitution of the United States provides
that the President shall be commander-in-chief
not only of the army but also of the navy. His
chief assistant in the management of naval affairs
is the Secretary of the Navy, who is also a member of his cabinet.

In 1898 the Navy Department of the United

States was just one hundred years old, having been organized in 1798 with Benjamin Stoddert as Secretary.

The work of the department is divided among eight bureaus, as follows:

1. The Bureau of Yards and Docks, which is intrusted with the construction and maintenance of docks and wharves, and with all civil engineering work in the navy yards.

2. The Bureau of Navigation, which superintends the education of officers and men, controls the enlistment of men and apprentices, and directs the movements of ships and fleets.

3. The Bureau of Equipment, which attends to the manufacture of ropes, anchors, cables, and other articles required for the equipment of naval vessels, purchases coal for their use, and controls the Naval Observatory.

4. The Bureau of Ordnance, which has charge of the manufacture of guns and ammunition, also of torpedo stations and magazines.

5. The Bureau of Construction and Repair, which is charged with the building and repair of

small boats and of the hulls of ships, and attends to the purchase of turrets and armor.

6. The Bureau of Steam Engineering, which directs the building and repairing of machinery in any way connected with the ships.

7. The Bureau of Medicine and Surgery, which designs, erects, and maintains naval hospitals and superintends their management.

8. The Bureau of Supplies and Accounts, which is responsible for the purchase and supply of all provisions and stores, and of the accounts relating to the same.

Each of these bureaus is presided over by an officer of skill and experience, who, while he holds the office, has the rank of commodore.

The United States has navy yards at Portsmouth, New Hampshire; Boston, Massachusetts; Brooklyn, New York; League Island, Pennsylvania; Norfolk, Virginia; Washington, District of Columbia; and Mare Island, California. At these navy yards ships are overhauled and repaired, machinery is adjusted and renewed, and stores of all kinds are provided. Here, too, on the receiving ships, the recruits are received and instructed.

There are naval stations at Newport, Rhode Island; New London, Connecticut; Port Royal, South Carolina; Key West and Pensacola, Florida; and Puget Sound, Washington.

At Indian Head, Maryland, is the naval proving-ground for the test of armor and guns.

The Naval Observatory is at Washington, and was at first merely a depot for naval charts and instruments.

In 1898, the highest officer in the American navy was the rear admiral. The other officers in their order, ranking downward, were commodores, captains, commanders, lieutenant commanders, lieutenants, lieutenants junior grade, and ensigns. All these are known as officers of the line.

At the close of the year there were seven rear admirals, ten commodores, forty-one captains, and eighty-five commanders.

The rank of rear admiral is equal to that of major general in the army. A commodore is equal to a brigadier general; a captain in the navy ranks with a colonel in the army; a commander ranks with a lieutenant colonel; and a lieutenant in the navy is equal to a captain in the army.

The law provides that when an officer reaches the age of sixty-two years he must be retired from active service. One who has been disabled in the service, or who has served honorably for forty years and requests release, may also be retired. Officers on the retired list receive three-fourths as much pay as when on active duty at sea.

Rear Admiral Dewey will be retired on the 26th of December, 1899. In 1898 there were thirty-three rear admirals on the retired lists.

The officers while at sea receive more pay than when on shore duty. The salary of an ensign at sea is $1200 a year; that of a rear admiral is $6,000. The salaries of the other officers range between these two extremes.

Previous to 1898 the number of enlisted men in the navy was limited to ten thousand. These men are received for a period of three years; and any one after serving continuously for twenty years may be assigned to duty in the navy yards, or on board receiving ships, or to other duties not requiring them to go far from home. All who have served thirty years are entitled to admittance in the Naval Home. The wages of enlisted men vary from $16 to $70 a month, according to the kind of work they perform.

The law provides that seven hundred and fifty boys may be enlisted as apprentices in the navy. These are received only with the consent of their parents or guardians, and are required to serve until they are twenty-one years old.

Besides the regular navy of the United States there is a naval militia organized in eighteen states. This militia is under the general direction of the Assistant Secretary of the Navy; and its duty in time of war is to man the vessels designed for coast and harbor defense.

At the beginning of the year 1898 there were more than four thousand men and officers in the naval militia. During the war with Spain, most of these were mustered into the naval service and did duty on the war vessels or in the signal service along the coast.

At the close of the year there were belonging to our government nine battleships, all of which had been built since 1890. Four others were in process of construction. The average cost of vessels of this class is about $3,500,000.

Of other vessels in the navy of 1898, there were two armored cruisers which cost $2,986,000 each; one ram, the *Katahdin;* six double turreted monitors; thirteen single turreted monitors; seventeen protected cruisers; four unarmored cruisers; fifteen gunboats ; and ten torpedo boats. Many other vessels of different classes were being built.

All these were in active service, or soon to be so. But there were also several other vessels of the old-fashioned style which, although of little use in battle, were valuable in the various peaceful enterprises in which the navy is always engaged. Of such there were six old iron vessels and ten wooden frigates, all propelled by steam, and seventeen old wooden sailing vessels, some of which were used as receiving ships.

During the war with Spain, many temporary additions were made to the navy. Eleven merchant vessels were bought or leased and converted into auxiliary cruisers. Among these were the four fast steamers of the American line, the *St. Louis*, the *St. Paul*, the *Yale*, and the *Harvard*.

Twenty-eight yachts also were purchased and turned into auxiliary gunboats or torpedo boats. Among these was the *Gloucester*, which did such fine work during the destruction of Cervera's fleet. It had formerly been a pleasure yacht belonging to Mr. J. Pierpont Morgan of New York.

In addition to the vessels just named, the government also bought twenty-seven tugs to be changed into gunboats or cruisers ; and it obtained seventeen steam vessels of various sizes to be used as transports and for many other purposes.

Altogether the navy of 1898 comprised an imposing collection of vessels of many kinds and of various degrees of efficiency. Of the work which it accomplished we have already learned.